Mighty Mentals

Book A

Peter Maher

Name ______________________________

Class ______________________________

Contents

Note to teachers and parents

Developing mental arithmetic skills

Automatic response—the ability to quickly recall basic mathematical facts, or to apply a known fact to a slightly modified situation or application—is an essential prerequisite for success in mathematics.

The development of modern technology and its applicability to the classroom in the form of the hand-held calculator has not diminished the significance of the role that mental arithmetic should play in schools. On the contrary, the advent of modern technology has increased the need for accurate mental arithmetic skill development in children. Without relatively accurate estimation prior to calculation, merely accepting at face value a solution on a screen can be fraught with danger. Inadvertently hitting the wrong buttons on a calculator is a commonly occurring fact of life. The result on the screen should never be blindly accepted. When we consider the fact that the great majority of the calculations secondary school students complete are done on the calculator, the validity of this point can be readily perceived.

By the end of primary school, a child should be in the habit of estimating and rounding off prior to using a calculator for computational purposes.

Appropriate estimation is reliant upon a sound knowledge of basic number facts, which should have been developed consistently throughout the primary years.

The better a student's abilities with mental arithmetic, the less time he or she will have to devote to looking up answers on a screen, in a book or on a chart. This point is demonstrated graphically with the game of 'beat the calculator'. Line up your students in pairs and tell them that some maths questions are going to be asked of the children who progressively come to the head of the line. Offer a calculator to one of the two students. Both will want it but only allow one to prevail. The other student will complain about how unfair the game is until the rules are made clear. The child with the calculator must press the appropriate buttons and display the correct answer. Ask the pairs of students questions they should be able to recall relatively quickly, such as 2 x 5 or 7 + 4. Now watch the child with the calculator complain that the game is unfair because the calculator is an encumbrance. Slip in the question 9 x 35 to see who is first with the correct answer. If the student using mental arithmetic is highly competent, 350 – 35 = 315 (10 lots of 35 minus one lot of 35) might still beat the calculator's 9 x 35 = 315.

It is also the case that the faster a student is with his or her basic number facts, the greater is the likelihood of structural computational success. Algorithms, such as long multiplication and division, contain numerous steps and stages. Students with inadequate mental arithmetic skills often take so long to recall a basic number fact that they forget the stage of the algorithm that they are progressing through. For these students the necessary foundation of times tables knowledge is inadequate—it is like trying to build on a foundation of sand. Without the necessary prerequisites of number facts competence, the algorithmic 'house' will tumble down.

It is invariably the case that the broader a student's body of mathematical knowledge, the more he or she will achieve in the subject and the more enjoyment that student will derive from the discipline. The message is clear: regularly practise automatic response games and activities, chants and rounds and all will benefit. Try to teach these number facts in as fun and meaningful a way as possible. Incorporate concrete materials and incentives into your number facts lessons.

Above all, teach for understanding. When teaching the 3 times table, show that the digits in the multiples will always sum to 3, 6 or 9. Show that the answers to the 9 times table always sum to 9. Show that adding on 8 is no harder than adding on 10—just jump back 2. Explain that the metric prefix 'kilo' stands for the number 1000, therefore there have to be 1000 grams in a kilogram and 1000 metres in a kilometre and, heaven forbid, 1000 tons of TNT in a kiloton bomb.

The patterns that make number-facts recall easy are out there and easy enough to find. Make the effort to demonstrate them at every possible opportunity. This book and the other books in this series will show you how.

How to use this book

The challenge of acquiring appropriate automatic response capabilities demands a structured and planned approach in schools. Mental arithmetic skills should be developed in a systematic manner over a period of years. The program should encompass the full range of the mathematics curriculum, covering measurement and space facts, data and chance questions as well as number problems.

The four books in this series assist with the development of mental arithmetic skills in a systematic and logical manner. Each book in the series contains 32 units of work. Each unit contains six sets of questions, which can represent one set per school day with one left over for homework. Alternatively, one day per week could be devoted to the completion of the six sets.

Each exercise in the books focuses on a specific concept, such as multiplying by 10, or the number of days in each month. The exercises have been set out in a logical sequence according to topic, for example bonding to 10 and adding on 10 should be taught and practised prior to adding on 9 or 11; digit recognition in place value should be completed prior to rounding off, and so on. However, the order in which the exercises are completed can be varied to suit the needs of your students. The exercises are at their most useful when linked to the topic under review in the classroom at the time.

The **Scope and Sequence Chart** on the inside front cover of this book will assist you to plan for the use of this book and to make it as relevant as possible to your students' individual learning capabilities.

At the top of each unit of work there is a **tip** for the students, to help them work through the exercises in that unit. At the bottom of each unit, you will find the relevant state **outcomes**.

The **Handy Maths Facts** on pages 4–5 are included as useful reference material for students.

How Well I Am Doing? on pages 6–7 affords the students the opportunity to record their scores on the unit exercises and to rate their own progress and performance.

A list of **answers** is found in the middle of each book and can be removed and stored if deemed appropriate.

The terms used in this book

The questions presented in this book utilise a wide variety of mathematical terms that are designed to reflect the structure of the discipline and to develop a student's mathematical vocabulary. Knowing, for example, that the terms 'add', 'sum', 'total' and 'altogether' all refer to the process of addition will have obvious benefits when a student has to tackle an addition problem set in context, or when problem solving.

A **Glossary** is provided on page 72 as a ready reference.

Handy Maths Facts

+ or −

	0	1	2	3	4	5	6	7	8	9	10	11	12
0	0	1	2	3	4	5	6	7	8	9	10	11	12
1	1	2	3	4	5	6	7	8	9	10	11	12	13
2	2	3	4	5	6	7	8	9	10	11	12	13	14
3	3	4	5	6	7	8	9	10	11	12	13	14	15
4	4	5	6	7	8	9	10	11	12	13	14	15	16
5	5	6	7	8	9	10	11	12	13	14	15	16	17
6	6	7	8	9	10	11	12	13	14	15	16	17	18
7	7	8	9	10	11	12	13	14	15	16	17	18	19
8	8	9	10	11	12	13	14	15	16	17	18	19	20
9	9	10	11	12	13	14	15	16	17	18	19	20	21
10	10	11	12	13	14	15	16	17	18	19	20	21	22
11	11	12	13	14	15	16	17	18	19	20	21	22	23
12	12	13	14	15	16	17	18	19	20	21	22	23	24

x or ÷

	0	1	2	3	4	5	6	7	8	9	10	11	12
0	0	0	0	0	0	0	0	0	0	0	0	0	0
1	0	1	2	3	4	5	6	7	8	9	10	11	12
2	0	2	4	6	8	10	12	14	16	18	20	22	24
3	0	3	6	9	12	15	18	21	24	27	30	33	36
4	0	4	8	12	16	20	24	28	32	36	40	44	48
5	0	5	10	15	20	25	30	35	40	45	50	55	60
6	0	6	12	18	24	30	36	42	48	54	60	66	72
7	0	7	14	21	28	35	42	49	56	63	70	77	84
8	0	8	16	24	32	40	48	56	64	72	80	88	96
9	0	9	18	27	36	45	54	63	72	81	90	99	108
10	0	10	20	30	40	50	60	70	80	90	100	110	120
11	0	11	22	33	44	55	66	77	88	99	110	121	132
12	0	12	24	36	48	60	72	84	96	108	120	132	144

Length

10 mm = 1 cm

1000 mm = 1 m

100 cm = 1 m

1000 m = 1 km

mm millimetre(s)

cm centimetre(s)

m metre(s)

km kilometre(s)

Mass

1000 g = 1 kg

1000 kg = 1 t

g gram(s)

kg kilogram(s)

t tonne(s)

Capacity

1000 mL = 1 L

1000 cm^3 = 1 L

1 cm^3 (water) weighs 1 g

mL millilitre(s)

L litre(s)

g gram(s)

cm^3 cubic centimetres

Time

60 seconds = 1 minute

60 minutes = 1 hour

24 hours = 1 day

7 days = 1 week

365 days = 1 year

366 days = 1 leap year

12 months = 1 year

10 years = 1 decade

100 years = 1 century

How well am I doing?

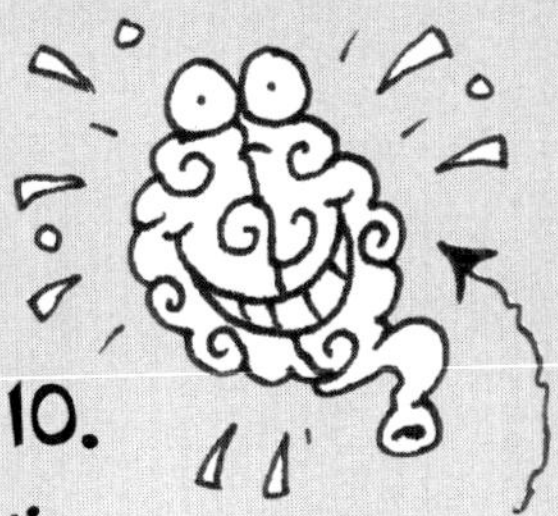

After you complete each set of work, fill in your score out of 10.
At the end of the six sets, rate yourself in the following way:
C = Can do better; I Improving; E = Excellent; or S = Superstar.

Unit	Topic	Set A	Set B	Set C	Set D	Set E	Set F	My Rating
1	Addition: Bonding to 10							
2	Addition: Adding on 10							
3	Addition: Adding on 9 or 11							
4	Subtraction: Subtracting from 10							
5	Subtraction: Subtracting 10, 9 or 11							
6	Doubling and near doubling							
7	Halving and near halving							
8	Multiplication: 2 times table							
9	Multiplication: 3 times table							
10	Multiplication: 4 times table							
11	Multiplication: 5 and 10 times tables							
12	Division: Dividing by 2							
13	Division: Dividing by 3							
14	Division: Dividing by 4							

Unit	Topic	Set A	Set B	Set C	Set D	Set E	Set F	My Rating
15	**Division:** Dividing by 5 and 10							
16	**Fractions:** Halves, quarters and parts of an amount							
17	**Place value:** Digit recognition							
18	**Rounding off:** Nearest 10 and 100							
19	**Sequences:** Finding missing terms							
20	**Number strings**							
21	**Length:** Units and conversions							
22	**Perimeter:** Concept and missing sides							
23	**Mass:** Units and conversions							
24	**Capacity/volume:** Units and conversions							
25	**Time:** Positions of the hands							
26	**Time:** Digital and analogue conversions							
27	**Time:** Unit equivalences							
28	**Money:** Notes and coins							
29	**Money:** Amounts, and adding and giving change							
30	**2D and 3D:** Polygon and polyhedra properties							
31	**Chance:** Concepts of likelihood							
32	**Revision:** All sorts							

Unit 1 Addition: Bonding to 10

Our number system is based on the number 10 because we have 10 fingers. See if you can bond to 10 quickly!

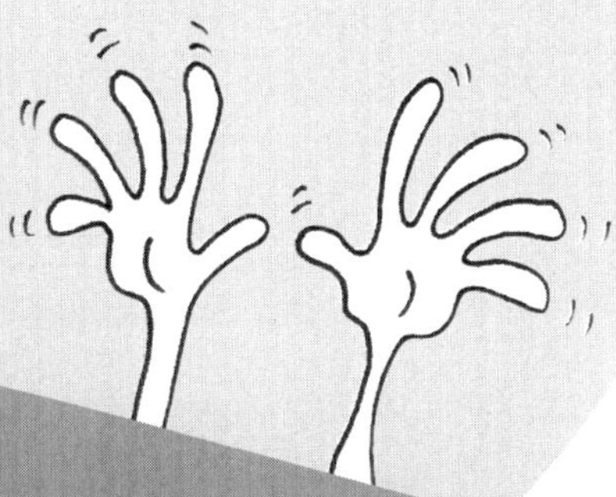

Set A

1 10 = 5 + ☐
2 10 = 9 + ☐
3 10 = 2 + ☐
4 10 = 6 + ☐
5 10 = 1 + ☐
6 10 = 3 + ☐
7 10 = 8 + ☐
8 10 = 7 + ☐
9 10 = 4 + ☐
10 10 = 0 + ☐

Set B

1 10 = 2 + 3 + ☐
2 10 = 5 + 1 + ☐
3 10 = 2 + 2 + ☐
4 10 = 3 + 3 + ☐
5 10 = 3 + 6 + ☐
6 10 = 1 + 1 + ☐
7 10 = 4 + 2 + ☐
8 10 = 5 + 4 + ☐
9 10 = 9 + 0 + ☐
10 10 = 7 + 1 + ☐

Set E

1 Find the sum of 6 and 4 ____
2 Find the sum of 8 and 2 ____
3 Add 3 to the total of 7 and 3 ____
4 What is 9 and 1 and 4 altogether? ____
5 What is 2 more than the sum of 8 and 2? ____
6 Add 7 to 4 and 6 ____
7 Add 8 to the sum of 9 and 1 ____
8 What is 5 and 5 and 6 altogether? ____
9 What is 6 greater than 8 plus 2? ____
10 Add 9 to the sum of 7 and 3 ____

Set C

1 10 = 2 + 2 + 2 + ☐

2 10 = 3 + 3 + 2 + ☐

3 10 = 1 + 1 + 2 + ☐

4 10 = 5 + 1 + 2 + ☐

5 10 = 4 + 4 + 1 + ☐

6 10 = 3 + 1 + 2 + ☐

7 10 = 2 + 3 + 4 + ☐

8 10 = 7 + 1 + 1 + ☐

9 10 = 0 + 0 + 5 + ☐

10 10 = 4 + 0 + 2 + ☐

Set D

What number is needed to make 10?

1 4 ☐

2 8 ☐

3 5 ☐

4 1 ☐

5 7 ☐

6 0 ☐

7 2 ☐

8 9 ☐

9 10 ☐

10 3 ☐

Set F

1 I need $10 and have saved $4. I still need to save $____

2 There are 10 stickers in a set. I have 8 and need ____ more.

3 We need 10 goals to win the game and have kicked 3. We need ____ more goals.

4 I made $10 with a $5 note, a $2 coin and ____ dollar coins.

5 I am missing 10 socks. I found 6. I still need to find ____ socks.

6 I need to do 10 sums for homework. I have completed 5. ____ more sums to go!

7 I must travel a journey of 10 stations on the train. I am at the 8th station. I have ____ stations to go.

8 I must clean 10 pairs of shoes. I have cleaned 8 pairs. ____ pairs to go!

9 I need 10 metres of fabric but only have 7 metres. I am short by ____ metres of fabric.

10 This is the last of these 10 questions. I have ____ left to do!

Unit 2 Addition: Adding on 10

Adding on 10 to a number is as simple as moving the tens place up 1. See how well you can do this with the following questions.

Set A

1 3 + 10 = ☐

2 5 + 10 = ☐

3 7 + 10 = ☐

4 0 + 10 = ☐

5 4 + 10 = ☐

6 6 + 10 = ☐

7 1 + 10 = ☐

8 9 + 10 = ☐

9 2 + 10 = ☐

10 8 + 10 = ☐

Set B

1 10 + 4 = ☐

2 10 + 8 = ☐

3 10 + 2 = ☐

4 10 + 5 = ☐

5 10 + 7 = ☐

6 10 + 1 = ☐

7 10 + 3 = ☐

8 10 + 6 = ☐

9 10 + 9 = ☐

10 10 + 0 = ☐

Set E

1 Find the sum of 33 and 10 ____

2 Add 87 to 10 ____

3 What is the total when 10 is added to 55? ____

4 What is 43 and 10 altogether? ____

5 What is the sum of 10 and 17? ____

6 Add 10 to 26 ____

7 Find the total of 68 and 10 ____

8 What is 10 more than the sum of 3 and 8? ____

9 Is the sum of 36 and 10 more than 45? ____

10 Is the total of 10 and 12 and 10 equal to 120? ____

Set C

1. 5 + 10 + 2 = ☐
2. 4 + 10 + 3 = ☐
3. 7 + 10 + 1 = ☐
4. 2 + 10 + 2 = ☐
5. 6 + 10 + 1 = ☐
6. 4 + 10 + 4 = ☐
7. 1 + 10 + 8 = ☐
8. 0 + 10 + 3 = ☐
9. 2 + 2 + 2 + 10 = ☐
10. 3 + 1 + 3 + 10 = ☐

Set D

1. 21 + 10 = ☐
2. 43 + 10 = ☐
3. 38 + 10 = ☐
4. 70 + 10 = ☐
5. 85 + 10 = ☐
6. 56 + 10 = ☐
7. 49 + 10 = ☐
8. 45 + 10 = ☐
9. 17 + 10 = ☐
10. 94 + 10 = ☐

Set F

1. I had 48 stickers and then was given 10 more. I now have ____ stickers.
2. Jack has 10 more stickers than the answer above. How many stickers does Jack have? ____
3. Sara has shot 87 netball goals. If she scores 10 more goals in her next game, her total goals will be ____ goals.
4. I saved $10 and was given $23. I then had $____.
5. Matthew scored 10 more runs than me. I scored 83 runs. He scored ____ runs.
6. I own 25 books. Elisa has 10 more books than me. She owns ____ books.
7. In the morning it was 10 degrees. Then it rose 11 degrees. The temperature was now ____ degrees.
8. I weigh 32 kilograms. My big sister weighs 10 kilograms more than me. She weighs ____ kilograms.
9. My team scored 29 points and lost by 10. Our opponents scored ____ points.
10. The pressure in my bike's rear tyre was 43 psi. My front tyre was 10 psi more than this. It's pressure was ____ psi.

Unit 3 Addition: Adding on 9 or 11

Adding on 9 or 11 is very similar to adding on 10. All you need to do is either add on 10 and jump back 1, or add on 10 and jump forward 1.

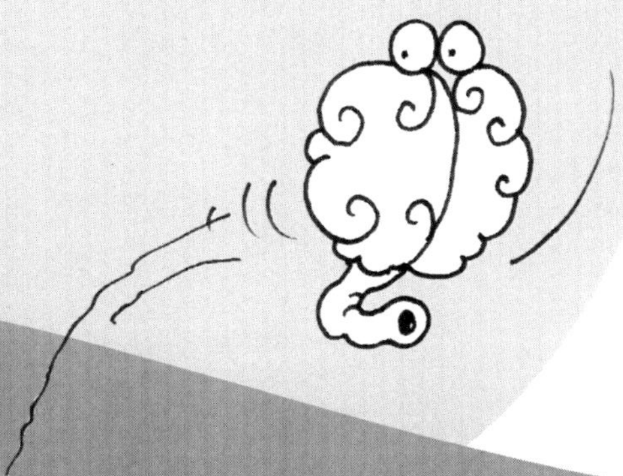

Set A

1. 7 + 9 = ☐
2. 5 + 9 = ☐
3. 1 + 9 = ☐
4. 6 + 9 = ☐
5. 3 + 9 = ☐
6. 0 + 9 = ☐
7. 2 + 9 = ☐
8. 8 + 9 = ☐
9. 4 + 9 = ☐
10. 9 + 9 = ☐

Set B

1. 3 + 11 = ☐
2. 8 + 11 = ☐
3. 2 + 11 = ☐
4. 7 + 11 = ☐
5. 9 + 11 = ☐
6. 1 + 11 = ☐
7. 10 + 11 = ☐
8. 5 + 11 = ☐
9. 0 + 11 = ☐
10. 4 + 11 = ☐

Set E

1. Add 9 on to 7 ____
2. Add 11 on to 55 ____
3. What is the sum of 34 and 9? ____
4. What is the sum of 72 and 11? ____
5. What is 49 and 9 altogether? ____
6. What is 48 and 11 altogether? ____
7. Find the total of 9 and 32 ____
8. Find the total of 83 and 11 ____
9. Is the sum of 75 and 9 more than 82? ____
10. Is the sum of 98 and 11 equal to 107? ____

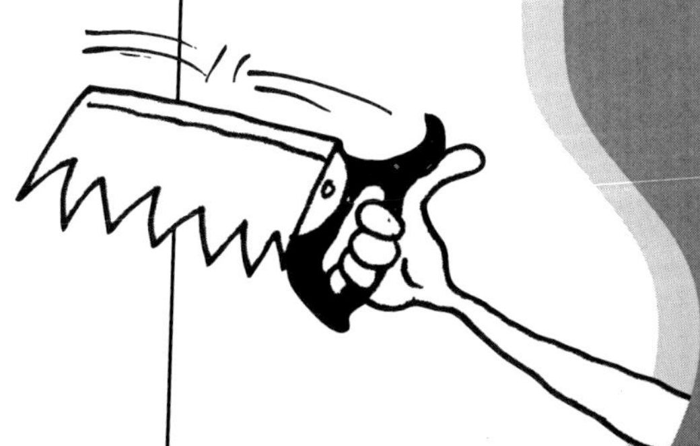

Set C

1 23 + 9 = ☐
2 84 + 9 = ☐
3 48 + 9 = ☐
4 17 + 9 = ☐
5 94 + 9 = ☐
6 33 + 9 = ☐
7 75 + 9 = ☐
8 40 + 9 = ☐
9 68 + 9 = ☐
10 57 + 9 = ☐

Set D

1 16 + 11 = ☐
2 83 + 11 = ☐
3 52 + 11 = ☐
4 92 + 11 = ☐
5 70 + 11 = ☐
6 29 + 11 = ☐
7 48 + 11 = ☐
8 66 + 11 = ☐
9 37 + 11 = ☐
10 9 + 11 = ☐

Set F

1 In the morning it was 9 degrees. It rose 9 more degrees in the afternoon. It was then ____ degrees.

2 It was 23 degrees in Sydney. It was 11 degrees hotter in Darwin. In Darwin it was ____ degrees.

3 My team scored 54 points but lost by 9 points. The winning team scored ____ points.

4 At half time in the netball the Swifts were 37 goals. They scored 11 goals in the third quarter. At three-quarter time they had scored ____ goals.

5 I owned 64 stamps and was given 9 more for my birthday. I now have ____ stamps.

6 My sister owns 11 more stamps than this total. How many does she own? ____

7 On Monday I saw 22 red cars on the way to school. I saw 9 more than this on Tuesday. On Tuesday I saw ____ red cars.

8 I have ridden 71 kilometres on my bike. My brother has ridden 11 kilometres more than me. He has ridden ____ kilometres on his bike.

9 I am 8 years old. My sister is 9 years older than me. She is ____ years old.

10 I live at 49 Cherry Street. My friend Jake lives in the same street and has a house number 11 bigger than mine. Jake lives at ____ Cherry Street.

Unit 4
Subtraction: Subtracting from 10

If you can bond to 10, taking away from 10 will be very easy. Just remember that subtraction is just the opposite to addition.

Set A

1 10 – 4 = ☐
2 10 – 9 = ☐
3 10 – 7 = ☐
4 10 – 3 = ☐
5 10 – 1 = ☐
6 10 – 8 = ☐
7 10 – 6 = ☐
8 10 – 0 = ☐
9 10 – 5 = ☐
10 10 – 2 = ☐

Set B

How many more do you need to take away from 10 to reach 0?

1 4 ☐
2 7 ☐
3 1 ☐
4 5 ☐
5 0 ☐
6 3 ☐
7 6 ☐
8 8 ☐
9 2 ☐
10 9 ☐

Set E

1 How many times can you take away 5 from 10? ____
2 How many times can 2 be taken away from 10? ____
3 How many times can you take away 1 from 10? ____
4 What is left over if you take 3, then 5 away from 10? ____
5 What is left over after taking away 3, twice, from 10? ____
6 Can you take 4 away from 10, 3 times? ____
7 Remove 7 from 10 and add on 2 ____
8 Remove 5 from 10 and add on 5 ____
9 Remove 2 from 10, 4 times ____
10 Remove 6 and then 2 and then 1 from 10 ____

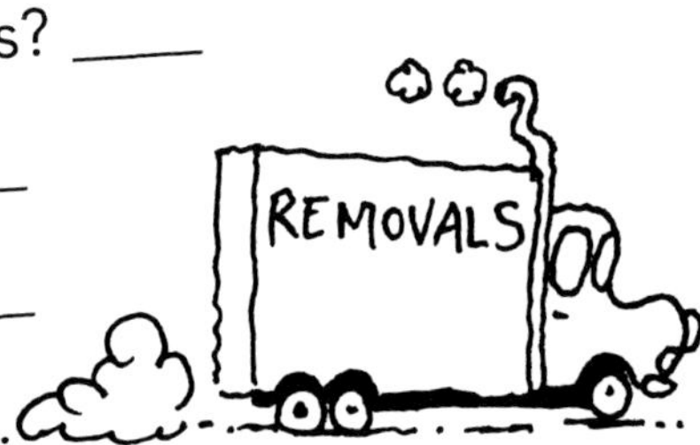

Set C

1 10 – 2 – 3 =

2 10 – 6 – 1 =

3 10 – 0 – 0 – 9 =

4 10 – 7 – 1 =

5 10 – 5 – 4 =

6 10 – 3 – 3 – 3 =

7 10 – 5 – 3 =

8 10 – 1 – 1 – 1 =

9 10 – 8 – 1 =

10 10 – 1 – 1 – 2 – 3 =

Set D

1 Subtract 5 from 10

2 Subtract 8 from 10

3 Take 2 away from 10

4 Take 9 away from 10

5 Take 7 away from 10

6 What is the difference between 10 and 2?

7 What is the difference between 10 and 0?

8 Subtract 4 and then 3 away from 10

9 Take 3 away twice from 10

10 Is the difference between 4 and 10 more than 5?

Set F

1 I had 10 coins and spent 4 of them. I had ____ coins left.

2 It was 10 degrees and then fell 7 degrees. It was then ____ degrees.

3 I put down 8 fingers. I had ____ fingers left standing up.

4 I can’t find 3 of my 10 socks. I can only find ____ socks.

5 My team scored 10 goals and I scored 2 of them. The rest of the team scored ____ goals between them.

6 I had to rule a 10 centimetre line, but my line was 3 centimetres short. My line was ____ centimetres long.

7 My birthday is on 10 May. Today is 8 May. I must wait ____ more days.

8 I want to lose 10 kilograms. I have already lost 7 kilograms. I must still lose ____ more kilograms.

9 Of the 10 shirts I own, 4 are too small. Only ____ fit me.

10 6 of my 10 video games are car racing games. ____ are not car racing games.

Number and Algebra

Unit 5
Subtraction: Subtracting 10, 9 or 11

When 10 is taken away from a number, like when we add on 10, we simply need to change the tens place—the units are not affected. Taking away 9 or 11 is as easy as taking away 10 and then either adding on 1 or taking 1 more away.

Set A

1. 15 – 10 = ☐
2. 23 – 10 = ☐
3. 45 – 10 = ☐
4. 82 – 10 = ☐
5. 98 – 10 = ☐
6. 37 – 10 = ☐
7. 48 – 10 = ☐
8. 90 – 10 = ☐
9. 21 – 10 = ☐
10. 74 – 10 = ☐

Set B

1. 54 – 9 = ☐
2. 74 – 9 = ☐
3. 12 – 9 = ☐
4. 39 – 9 = ☐
5. 78 – 9 = ☐
6. 51 – 9 = ☐
7. 47 – 9 = ☐
8. 38 – 9 = ☐
9. 17 – 9 = ☐
10. 80 – 9 = ☐

Set E

1. What is the difference between 38 and 10? ____
2. What is the difference between 97 and 9? ____
3. What is the difference between 73 and 11? ____
4. Take 9 away from 30 ____
5. Take 11 away from 49 ____
6. Take 10 away from 22 ____
7. Reduce 54 by 11 ____
8. Reduce 92 by 9 ____
9. Reduce 64 by 10 ____
10. Subtract 10 and then 11, from 99 ____

Set C

1 32 – 11 =

2 74 – 11 =

3 59 – 11 =

4 20 – 11 =

5 27 – 11 =

6 84 – 11 =

7 80 – 11 =

8 28 – 11 =

9 73 – 11 =

10 90 – 11 =

Set D

1 53 – 10 =

2 86 – 9 =

3 27 – 11 =

4 93 – 9 =

5 38 – 9 =

6 72 – 10 =

7 45 – 11 =

8 32 – 10 =

9 31 – 11 =

10 40 – 9 =

Set F

1 James ran 42 kilometres in the marathon. Stewart ran 11 kilometres less than James. Stewart ran ____ kilometres.

2 I can run 100 metres in 19 seconds. The world record is about 9 seconds faster than this. The world record is about ____ seconds.

3 I live 13 train stations from the city. I have passed 10 stations. ____ stations to go.

4 Claire wants to buy a new toy horse, which costs $34. She still needs to save another $11. Claire has saved $____.

5 The Stingrays scored 35 goals and beat us by 9 goals. We scored ____ goals.

6 The Bullets scored 27 points and won by a margin of 10. Their opposition scored ____ points.

7 The margin between 2 cricket teams was 11 runs. The winners scored 98 runs. The beaten team scored ____ runs.

8 I need a ribbon that is 84 centimetres long, but the one I have is 10 centimetres too short. The ribbon I have is ____ centimetres long.

9 The bus I catch is due at 10:54. It is now 10:43. It is due in ____ minutes.

10 I own 34 stickers. Sam owns 43 stickers. Sam owns ____ more stickers than me.

Number and Algebra

Unit 6 Doubling and near doubling

Knowing how to add a number onto itself (doubling) is a very useful skill and helps when adding up. If you know the 2 times table, you can double numbers. Near doubling just needs a little extra step.

Set A

1. 3 + 3 = ☐
2. 8 + 8 = ☐
3. 2 + 2 = ☐
4. 9 + 9 = ☐
5. 0 + 0 = ☐
6. 7 + 7 = ☐
7. 1 + 1 = ☐
8. 5 + 5 = ☐
9. 6 + 6 = ☐
10. 4 + 4 = ☐

Set B

1. 5 + 4 = ☐
2. 7 + 6 = ☐
3. 8 + 7 = ☐
4. 2 + 1 = ☐
5. 4 + 3 = ☐
6. 6 + 5 = ☐
7. 1 + 0 = ☐
8. 10 + 9 = ☐
9. 9 + 8 = ☐
10. 3 + 2 = ☐

Set E

1. Double 5 and add on 3 ____
2. Double 3 and double it again ____
3. Double 8 and take away 3 ____
4. Take 5. Double it and then add on 8 ____
5. Reduce 10 by 3 doubled ____
6. Which number, when doubled and doubled again, equals 12? ____
7. Take 10 away from 6 doubled ____
8. Double 4. Add on 3. Double this ____
9. What is the difference between 4 doubled and 6 doubled? ____
10. Reduce 5 doubled by 2 doubled ____

Set C

1. 5 + 6 = ☐
2. 2 + 3 = ☐
3. 10 + 11 = ☐
4. 4 + 5 = ☐
5. 7 + 8 = ☐
6. 9 + 10 = ☐
7. 6 + 7 = ☐
8. 3 + 4 = ☐
9. 8 + 9 = ☐
10. 1 + 2 = ☐

Set D

1. Double 7 ☐
2. Which number, when doubled, equals 18? ☐
3. Double 1 ☐
4. Which number, when doubled, equals 8? ☐
5. Double 8 ☐
6. Which number, when doubled, equals 6? ☐
7. Double 6 ☐
8. Which number, when doubled, equals 10? ☐
9. Double 2 ☐
10. Which number, when doubled, equals 20? ☐

Set F

1. I ran 7 kilometres. Jack ran twice this distance. How far did Jack run? ____ kilometres.
2. I kicked 22 goals last season, which was twice as many as Stella kicked. How many goals did Stella kick last season? ____ goals.
3. Caitlin has $12 in her purse. I have twice as much as this in my purse. I have $ ____
4. My cards add up to 9 points. David's cards add up to twice this total. They add up to ____ points.
5. Luke can swim 25 metres in 22 seconds. This is twice the club record for 25 metres. The club record for 25 metres is ____ seconds.
6. A bag of potatoes weighs 8 kilograms. 2 bags of potatoes weigh ____ kilograms.
7. I owned 6 model cars but, last Christmas, I was given this number again. I now own ____ model cars.
8. In my new novel I am up to page 12. I am twice as far into the book as Sue. She is up to page ____.
9. In the tennis championships, Claire won 18 games, which was twice as many games as her opponent. Her opponent won ____ games.
10. In the little athletics championships my club won 16 gold medals. This was twice as many as our previous record. Our previous record was ___ gold medals.

Number and Algebra

Unit 7 Halving and near halving

If you can double a number, then you can halve it as well, because one is the opposite of the other. It's like saying that if you can add, you must be able to subtract as well, because they are opposites too.

Set A

Halve these numbers:

1. 14 ☐
2. 8 ☐
3. 10 ☐
4. 2 ☐
5. 18 ☐
6. 6 ☐
7. 16 ☐
8. 20 ☐
9. 12 ☐
10. 4 ☐

Set B

1. 18 – 9 = ☐
2. 12 – 6 = ☐
3. 10 – 5 = ☐
4. 8 – 4 = ☐
5. 24 – 12 = ☐
6. 22 – 11 = ☐
7. 4 – 2 = ☐
8. 14 – 7 = ☐
9. 20 – 10 = ☐
10. 6 – 3 = ☐

Set E

1. Find half of 6 ____
2. What is half of 24? ____
3. Is 7 half of 16? ____
4. Find half of 22 ____
5. Is 9 half of 18? ____
6. Halve 18 ____
7. Halve 20 and add on 3 ____
8. Halve 24, then halve it again ____
9. Take 2 away from half of 16 ____
10. Double a half of 10 ____

Set C

Write 'more' if the number in brackets is more than half of the given number or 'less' if it is less than half of the given number.

1 14 (6) ______
2 22 (12) ______
3 6 (4) ______
4 18 (7) ______
5 4 (3) ______
6 12 (7) ______
7 24 (10) ______
8 8 (3) ______
9 10 (4) ______
10 16 (7) ______

Set D

What is half the number?

1	12	☐
2	32	☐
3	28	☐
4	8	☐
5	36	☐
6	40	☐
7	48	☐
8	2	☐
9	0	☐
10	16	☐

Set F

1 I spelt correctly half of the 14 words on the spelling test. I spelt ____ words correctly.

2 We kicked 22 goals and our opponents only kicked half as many goals. They kicked ____ goals.

3 I had $20 and spent half of this on lollies. I had $____ left.

4 2 bags of onions weigh 12 kilograms and I am carrying 1 bag. I am carrying ____ kilograms.

5 There are 24 children in my class. Half learn a musical instrument. How many children do not learn a musical instrument? ____

6 I take size 10 in shoes. My little sister takes half this size. She wears size ____ shoes.

7 I had 16 shots at goal but only half of the shots were successful. I shot ____ goals.

8 Last season 18 catches came my way. I held half of them. I took ____ catches last season.

9 My dad pays $4.20 on the bus. I pay half fare. A ticket costs me $____.

10 There are 8 states or territories in Australia. Half are bigger than New South Wales. ____ states and territories are bigger than NSW.

Number and Algebra

Unit 8
Multiplication: 2 times table

Numbers in the 2 times table are always even and end in a 0, 2, 4, 6 or 8. The skills you developed in the doubling unit of work will help you to find the answers to the following questions.

Set A

Which of these numbers are even and will be in the 2 times table? Write 'yes' if the number is in the 2 times table and 'no' if it is not.

1 8 ____
2 17 ____
3 23 ____
4 18 ____
5 21 ____
6 13 ____
7 20 ____
8 14 ____
9 16 ____
10 22 ____

Set B

Write 'even' next to all the even numbers and 'odd' next to all the odd numbers.

1 56 ____
2 78 ____
3 91 ____
4 177 ____
5 323 ____
6 430 ____
7 747 ____
8 784 ____
9 132 ____
10 999 ____

Set E

1 Multiply 6 by 2 ____
2 What is the product of 8 and 2? ____
3 How many groups of 2 make 18? ____
4 Is 143 an even number? ____
5 What is 5 times 2? ____
6 What is the product of 11 and 2? ____
7 What is the answer to 5 + 5, multiplied by 2? ____
8 Multiply 6 by 2 and double the answer ____
9 Take 9 from 12 and then multiply this by 2 ____
10 2 x 2 x 2 x 2 = ____

Set C

Multiply these numbers by 2:

1	4	
2	9	
3	5	
4	7	
5	1	
6	8	
7	3	
8	11	
9	10	
10	0	

Set D

How many 2s will equal these numbers?

1	24	
2	16	
3	8	
4	20	
5	2	
6	10	
7	18	
8	0	
9	22	
10	14	

Set F

1 Jack has twice the number of lollies that I do. I have 7. Jack has ___ lollies.

2 I scored 8 netball goals today. Last weekend, I scored twice as many as this. Last weekend I scored ___ goals.

3 It is currently 5 degrees and is expected to get to twice this temperature. It is expected to reach ___ degrees.

4 On the weekend, 3 buses an hour go past my house. This figure doubles on weekdays. On weekdays, ___ buses an hour go past my house.

5 Stephanie owns 2 times the number of pets that I own. I own 8 pets. Stephanie owns ___ pets.

6 I have read 11 pages of my novel. Cory reads twice as quickly as me. She has just finished page ___.

7 I own 8 pairs of shoes. I own ___ shoes altogether.

8 If I multiply the number of dollars I own by 2, I would have $100. I currently own $___.

9 Our team has scored 20 runs. We must score twice this number of runs to reach our opponent's total. They scored ___ runs.

10 I set the table with a knife and a fork for 4 people. I used ___ pieces of cutlery.

NSW: Number NS2.3; Qld: Number concepts N3.3; Vic: Mental computation and estimation 3.1; WA: Number N3.3; SA: Number 2.8

Number and Algebra

Unit 9
Multiplication: 3 times table

The digits of all numbers in the 3 times table sum to 3, 6 or 9. So, the number 24 is in the 3 times table because the tens and the units places add up to 6. In the number 99 the tens and the units places add up to 18, and 1 and 8 add up to 9.

For Sets A and B, write 'yes' next to the numbers with digits that sum to 3, 6 or 9 and 'no' next to those that don't.

Set A

1	**27**	☐
2	**31**	☐
3	**15**	☐
4	**30**	☐
5	**17**	☐
6	**32**	☐
7	**33**	☐
8	**52**	☐
9	**11**	☐
10	**23**	☐

Set B

1	**64**	☐
2	**40**	☐
3	**39**	☐
4	**82**	☐
5	**48**	☐
6	**66**	☐
7	**91**	☐
8	**84**	☐
9	**55**	☐
10	**75**	☐

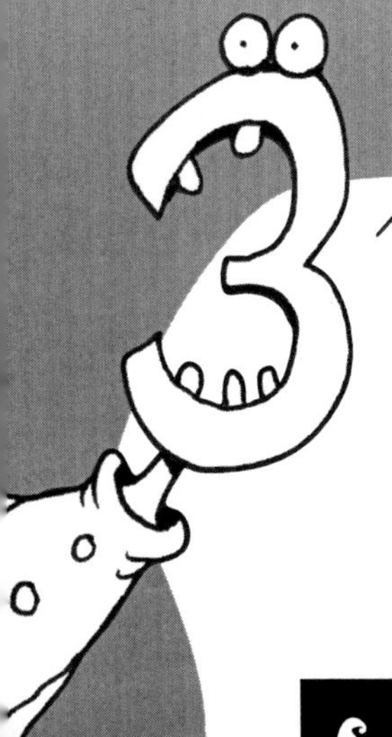

Set E

1 Find the product of 3 and 7 ____

2 What is 3 multiplied by 9? ____

3 5 groups of 3 make ____

4 8 times 3 equals ____

5 Find the product of 3 and 11 ____

6 What is the answer to 6 multiplied by 3? ____

7 Zero threes equal ____

8 12 groups of 3 is more than 40. True, or false? ____

9 2 x 3 x 3 = ____

10 10 x 3 x 2 = ____

Set C

1	3 x 3 =	
2	8 x 3 =	
3	11 x 3 =	
4	10 x 3 =	
5	6 x 3 =	
6	1 x 3 =	
7	12 x 3 =	
8	0 x 3 =	
9	7 x 3 =	
10	5 x 3 =	

How many groups of 3 make these numbers?

Set D

1	9	
2	12	
3	27	
4	15	
5	33	
6	6	
7	18	
8	36	
9	21	
10	3	

Set F

1 I kicked 4 goals for my team last week. So far this season I have kicked 3 times as many goals as this. This season I have kicked ____ goals.

2 If I tripled the number of dolls I own, I would have 12 dolls. Now I own ____ dolls.

3 1 banana costs 11 cents. 3 bananas cost ____ cents.

4 My little brother owns 5 tricycles. Altogether, these tricycles have ____ wheels.

5 How many horns would be on the faces of 7 toy triceratops? ____

6 How many legs are on 10 tripods? ____

7 How many stumps in 3 sets of cricket stumps? ____

8 Emma shot 8 three pointers in her last basketball game. This was equal to ____ points for her team.

9 An apple costs 12 cents. 3 apples cost ____ cents.

10 How many months in 9 seasons? ____

Number and Algebra

Unit 10 Multiplication: 4 times table

All numbers in the 4 times table have to be even, because these numbers are also in the 2 times table. However, be careful! Only every second number in the 2 times table is in the 4 times table. For example, 2 isn't, 4 is, 6 isn't, 8 is, and so on.

Set A

Circle the numbers that could not possibly be in the 4 times table:

11 72 56 92 77 87 88 89 129 232

64 74 23 81 24 85 70 121 68 47

Set B

Circle the numbers that are in the 4 times table:

2 4 6 8 10 12 14 16 18 20 22

24 26 28 30 32 34 36 38 40

Set E

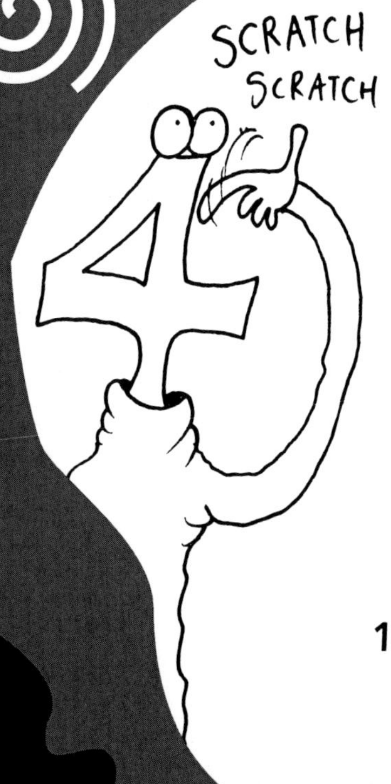

1 How many groups of 4 equal 28? ____

2 Find the product of 11 and 4 ____

3 Quadruple 8 ____

4 Zero times 4 equals ____

5 Multiply 6 by 4 ____

6 Find the product of 2 and 4 ____

7 What is the result when 9 is multiplied by 4? ____

8 Quadruple 5 ____

9 Multiply 7 by 4 and then add 10 ____

10 Find the answer to 4 multiplied by itself ____.

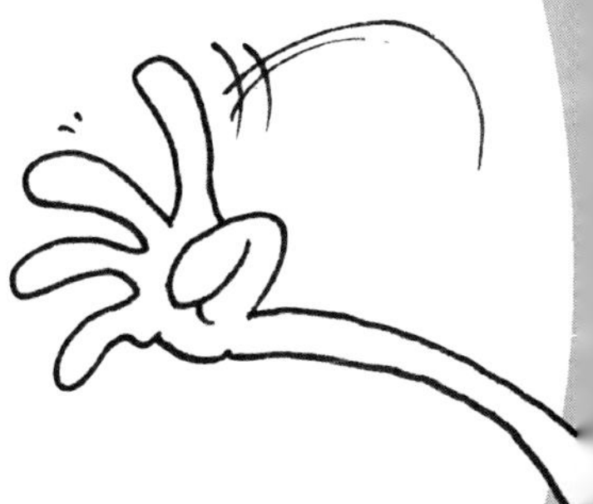

Set C

1	3 x 4 =	☐
2	8 x 4 =	☐
3	11 x 4 =	☐
4	9 x 4 =	☐
5	12 x 4 =	☐
6	6 x 4 =	☐
7	0 x 4 =	☐
8	2 x 4 =	☐
9	10 x 4 =	☐
10	5 x 4 =	☐

Set D

How many groups of 4 make these numbers?

1	24	☐
2	12	☐
3	44	☐
4	4	☐
5	48	☐
6	0	☐
7	32	☐
8	16	☐
9	36	☐
10	28	☐

Set F

1 In the morning it was only 4 degrees, but during the day it was 4 times as warm. The top temperature for the day was ____ degrees.

2 My friend Laura owns 6 horses. The horses have ____ legs altogether.

3 How many seasons in 10 years? ____

4 I am up to page 7 in my book. It is 4 times as long as this. The book is ____ pages long.

5 I own a dog, a cat and 9 mice. They have ____ legs altogether.

6 I struck 5 fours and then was out. I scored ____ runs.

7 I am at school for about 6 hours. A day is 4 times as long as this. A day contains ____ hours.

8 How many Jacks, Queens and Kings are in a deck of cards altogether? ____

9 How many quarters in 8 games of football? ____

10 My big brother is 12 years old. My dad is 4 times as old as this. My Dad is ____ years old.

NSW: Number NS2.3; Qld: Number concepts N3.3;
Vic: Mental computation and estimation 3.1; WA: Number N3.3; SA: Number 2.8

Number and Algebra

Unit 11
Multiplication: The 5 times and 10 times tables

Numbers in the 5 times table end in either a 5 or a 0. Numbers in the 10 times table end in a 0. So, if a number ends in a 7, it will be 2 past a number in the 5 times table or 7 past a number in the 10 times table.

Set A

Circle the numbers that could not be in the 5 times or 10 times tables:

11 75 70 23 48 65 93 772 800 725

27 80 100 81 64 89 20 73 35 95

Set B

How far past a number in the 5 times table are the following numbers?

1	**22**	☐
2	**46**	☐
3	**78**	☐
4	**49**	☐
5	**93**	☐
6	**146**	☐
7	**544**	☐
8	**788**	☐
9	**566**	☐
10	**129**	☐

Set E

1. What is the product of 6 and 5? ____
2. Multiply 10 by itself ____
3. 11 groups of 5 equal ____
4. 2 times 5 times 10 equals ____
5. What is 8 times 5? ____
6. Add 10 to the product of 10 and 3 ____
7. How many past a number in the 5 times table is the number 58? ____
8. What is the closest number in the 10 times table to 73? ____
9. Double the product of 5 and 10 ____
10. Reduce 9 x 10 by twenty ____

Set C

How far past a number in the 10 times table are these numbers?

1. 13 ☐
2. 27 ☐
3. 35 ☐
4. 48 ☐
5. 66 ☐
6. 79 ☐
7. 93 ☐
8. 106 ☐
9. 111 ☐
10. 123 ☐

Set D

1. 4 x 5 = ☐
2. 6 x 10 = ☐
3. 8 x 5 = ☐
4. 12 x 10 = ☐
5. 5 x 5 = ☐
6. 4 x 10 = ☐
7. 9 x 5 = ☐
8. 11 x 10 = ☐
9. 7 x 5 = ☐
10. 10 x 10 = ☐

Set F

1. A pentagon has 5 sides. How many sides in 8 pentagons? _____
2. A squid has 10 legs. How many legs on 10 squids? ____
3. It was 3 degrees this morning and rose to be 5 times as warm in the afternoon. In the afternoon it was ____ degrees.
4. How many sides on 8 decagons? ____
5. My little sister is 7 years old. My mum is 5 times this age. She is ____ years old.
6. I am 9 years old. My great-grandfather is 10 times as old as me. He is ____ years old.
7. Jade runs 5 kilometres every day for cross-country training. Last week she ran ____ kilometres.
8. A heptagon has 7 sides. How many sides in 10 heptagons? ____ sides.
9. I saved six $5 notes. I have $ ____ altogether.
10. My uncle is as old as 4 decades. He is ____ years old.

Unit 12 Division: Dividing by 2

Dividing means to break up into equal pieces. Dividing by 2 is the same as halving, or to break something up into 2 equal pieces. Dividing is the opposite of multiplying. If you can multiply by 2, you can divide by 2 just as easily. Division is also a quick way of subtracting over and over again. So, 10 divided by 2 really means 'How many times can you take away 2 from 10?'

Set A

Which of these numbers will divide by 2 and not leave a remainder? Circle them.

6 13 17 22 8 19 21 20 10 7 39

18 53 81 34 56 45 97 12 48

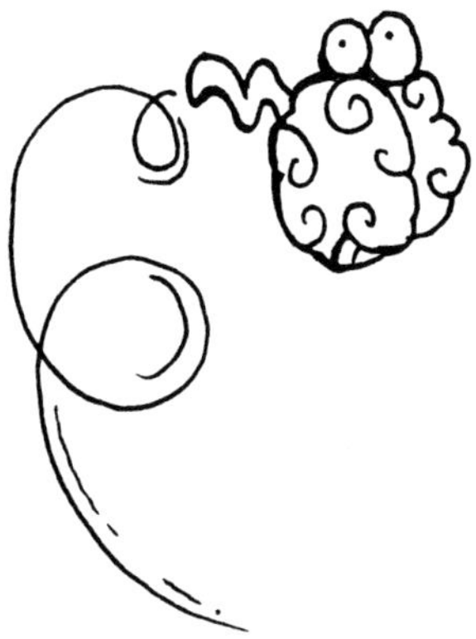

Set B

Divide these numbers by 2:

1	14	
2	22	
3	6	
4	10	
5	24	
6	2	
7	12	
8	4	
9	8	
10	20	

Set E

1. Divide 20 by 2 ____
2. What is the quotient of 14 and 2? ____
3. How many times will 2 divide into 16? ____
4. Split 22 into 2 equal groups ____
5. Divide 18 by 2 ____
6. What is the answer to 2 divided by 2? ____
7. What is the remainder when 23 is divided by 2? ____
8. Does 2 divide into 10 without a remainder? ____
9. Divide 20 by 2 and then by 2 again ____
10. What is the remainder when 12 is divided by 2? ____

Set C

Which numbers have been divided by 2 to produce these answers?

1	3	☐
2	7	☐
3	10	☐
4	8	☐
5	1	☐
6	6	☐
7	2	☐
8	5	☐
9	4	☐
10	12	☐

Set D

Answer 'true' or 'false':

1 $22 \div 2 = 11$ ______
2 $12 \div 2 = 6$ ______
3 $14 \div 2 = 8$ ______
4 $18 \div 2 = 7$ ______
5 $20 \div 2 = 10$ ______
6 $23 \div 2 = 12$ ______
7 $6 \div 2 = 4$ ______
8 $16 \div 2 = 8$ ______
9 $14 \div 2 = 7$ ______
10 $12 \div 2 = 6$ ______

Set F

1 Ben and Sean shared 14 marbles equally. They received ____ marbles each.

2 A dollar split into 2 equal parts gives 2 _____ coins.

3 I had to share my 24 horse stickers equally with my sister. We then had ____ stickers each.

4 In the cricket match the 10 wickets were shared equally between 2 bowlers. They took ____ wickets each.

5 I had 16 shots at goal. These shots were equally split between goals and behinds. How many goals did I score? ____.

6 18 votes were cast for house captain and the 2 girls standing each received the same number of votes. The 2 girls each received ____ votes.

7 I was asked to share $12 equally with my brother. We received $____ each.

8 Our goal shooter and goal attack, between them, scored 22 goals in the netball match. They scored the same number of goals. Each scored ____ goals.

9 Can seven $1 coins be shared equally between 2 children? ____

10 Why or why not? ____

Number and Algebra

Unit 13 Division: Dividing by 3

When we divide a number or an amount by **3**, it is the opposite of multiplying by **3**. If **12** is divided by **3**, or split into **3** equal parts, we count in groups of **3** until we reach **12**: **3**, 6, 9, 12 = 4 groups; and so, 12 split into **3** equal parts equals 4.

Remember that if a number can be divided by **3** without a remainder, it must be in the **3** times table, with its digits summing to either **3**, 6 or 9.

Set A

Which of these numbers could be divided by 3 without giving a remainder? Circle them.

15 33 31 13 27 37 24 28 9 111

63 72 38 26 45 20 42 19 22 34

Set B

Divide these numbers by 3:

1 **9** ☐
2 **18** ☐
3 **30** ☐
4 **12** ☐
5 **3** ☐
6 **21** ☐
7 **36** ☐
8 **15** ☐
9 **0** ☐
10 **24** ☐

Set E

1 Divide 27 by 3 ____
2 What is the quotient of 33 and 3? ____
3 How many times could 3 be taken away from 21? ____
4 Divide 18 by 3 ____
5 Split 12 into 3 equal pieces ____
6 What is the quotient of 9 and 3? ____
7 How many times can 3 be taken away from 15? ____
8 Split 24 into 3 equal pieces ____
9 What is the remainder when 22 is divided by 3? ____
10 What number has been divided by 3 to produce 10? ____

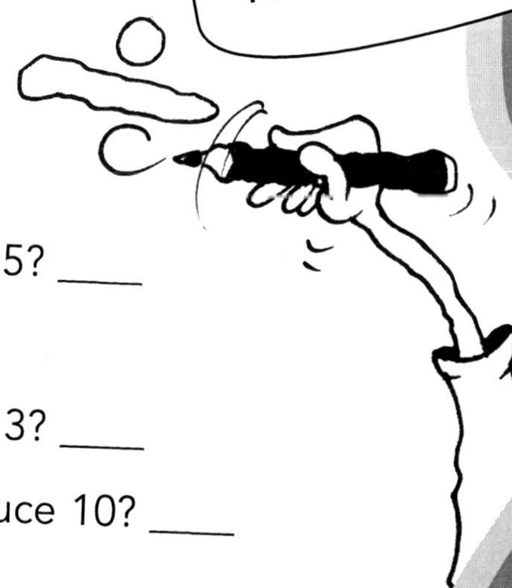

Set C

Which numbers have been divided by 3 to produce the following answers?

1	6	☐
2	2	☐
3	11	☐
4	1	☐
5	8	☐
6	10	☐
7	7	☐
8	0	☐
9	4	☐
10	9	☐

Set D

What will the remainders be when these numbers are divided by 3?

1	4	☐
2	11	☐
3	21	☐
4	17	☐
5	31	☐
6	18	☐
7	8	☐
8	27	☐
9	24	☐
10	29	☐

Set F

1 My triangles have 6 sides altogether. How many triangles do I have? ____

2 The 21 children in the class were divided into 3 teams. There were ____ children in each team.

3 My basketball three pointers were worth 33 points for my team. I scored ____ three pointers.

4 9 months equals ____ seasons.

5 I shared $18 equally with my 2 sisters. We each received $____.

6 In the last 3 games, my rugby team has scored a total of 24 points and scored the same number of points in each game. In each game we scored ____ points.

7 My triceratops models have 12 horns altogether. I own ____ triceratops models.

8 In my piggy bank I have a total of $30 in $10 notes. I have ____ $10 notes in my piggy bank.

9 A yard was an old measure of about a metre and each yard was equal to 3 feet. 15 feet was equal to ____ yards.

10 In the first 27 days of this month it has rained every third day. This month it has rained on ____ days.

Number and Algebra

Unit 14 Division: Dividing by 4

Set A

Which of these numbers, when divided by 4, could not possibly leave a whole number with no remainder? Circle them.

44 31 77 24 42 69 121 80 235 212

23 88 37 19 92 100 251 93 120 52

Remember that to divide by 4 is the exact opposite of multiplying by 4. If 4 groups of 3 equal 12, then 12 divided by 3 must equal 4. If a number is divisible by 4, it must be even.

Set B

Divide these numbers by 4:

1	28	
2	40	
3	8	
4	12	
5	20	
6	4	
7	16	
8	24	
9	36	
10	48	

Set E

1 What is the quotient of 44 and 4? ____

2 Divide 32 by 4 ____

3 How many fours will go into 24? ____

4 How many times can 4 be taken away from 16? ____

5 What is the remainder when 41 is divided by 4? ____

6 Which number, when divided by 4 and then by 4 again, will give 1 as the answer? ____

7 Divide 48 by 4 and then remove 2 from the answer ____

8 What is the closest number to 35 that can be divided by 4 without a remainder? ____

9 Find the quotient of 32 and 4 and add 10 to the result ____

10 Divide 40 by the sum of 2 and 2 ____

Set C

Which numbers have been divided by 4 to produce these answers?

1	5	
2	9	
3	3	
4	0	
5	11	
6	2	
7	10	
8	7	
9	6	
10	4	

Set D

What is the remainder when these numbers are divided by 4?

1	11	
2	7	
3	10	
4	22	
5	31	
6	6	
7	39	
8	27	
9	46	
10	29	

Set F

1 8 pies were shared among 4 families. Each family received ____ pies.

2 I own toy horses which, altogether, have 24 legs. I own ____ toy horses.

3 The squares in my set of blocks have 16 sides. There are ____ squares in my set.

4 I have a dozen eggs and will make cakes that require 4 eggs each. I will bake ____ cakes.

5 The 48 children in Year 3 were split into 4 houses. Each house has ____ children in it.

6 36 Easter eggs were shared among 4 children. Each received ____ eggs.

7 Farmer Brown owns pigs that have a total of 40 legs altogether. Farmer Brown owns ____ pigs.

8 It has been wet on every fourth day this month. We are at day 20 of the month. Is it wet today? ____

9 Can I equally share 42 lollies with my 3 best friends? ____

10 I have played 4 quarters of football. I have played in ____ whole game of football.

Unit 15 Division: Dividing by 5 and 10

Dividing by 5 or by 10 means to split something into 5 or 10 equal pieces. If a number can be divided by 5,with no remainder, it must be in the 5 times table and end in either a 5 or a 0. If it ends in a 6 or a 1, it must have a remainder of 1 when divided by 5. If it ends in a 7 or a 2, it must have a remainder of 2 when divided by 5, and so on. If a number ends in a 4, when divided by 10, it will leave 4 as a remainder. If it ends in an 8, it will leave 8 as a remainder when divided by 10, and so on.

Set A

Which of these numbers are not in the 5 or 10 times tables? Circle them.

23 75 245 80 92 120 330 789 57 375

79 43 67 90 45 98 65 101 86 125

Set B

What is the remainder when these numbers are divided by 5?

1	**23**	☐
2	**19**	☐
3	**36**	☐
4	**40**	☐
5	**61**	☐
6	**82**	☐
7	**8**	☐
8	**94**	☐
9	**85**	☐
10	**77**	☐

Set E

1 Divide 35 by 5 ____

2 What is the quotient of 60 and 10? ____

3 How many times can 5 be subtracted from 20? ____

4 What is the remainder when 47 is divided by 10? ____

5 Can 54 be divided by 5 with no remainder? ____

6 How many tens go into 30? _____

7 Can 55 pieces of paper be shared equally among 5 people? ____

8 Divide 50 by 5 and then by 10 ____

9 Take 4 away from the quotient of 40 and 5 ____

10 How many tens will divide into a half of 60? ____

Answers

Unit 1 Addition: Bonding to 10

	Set A	Set B	Set C	Set D	Set E	Set F
1	5	5	4	6	10	$6
2	1	4	2	2	10	2
3	8	6	6	5	13	7
4	4	4	2	9	14	3 dollar coins
5	9	1	1	3	12	4
6	7	8	4	10	17	5
7	2	4	1	8	18	2
8	3	1	1	1	16	2
9	6	1	5	0	16	3
10	10	2	4	7	19	0

Unit 2 Addition: Adding on 10

	Set A	Set B	Set C	Set D	Set E	Set F
1	13	14	17	31	43	58
2	15	18	17	53	97	68
3	17	12	18	48	65	97
4	10	15	14	80	53	$33
5	14	17	17	95	27	93
6	16	11	18	66	36	35
7	11	13	19	59	78	21
8	19	16	13	55	21	42
9	12	19	16	27	yes	39
10	18	10	17	104	no	53

Unit 3 Addition: Adding on 9 or 11

	Set A	Set B	Set C	Set D	Set E	Set F
1	16	14	32	27	16	18
2	14	19	93	94	66	34
3	10	13	57	63	43	63
4	15	18	26	103	83	48
5	12	20	103	81	58	73
6	9	12	42	40	59	84
7	11	21	84	59	41	31
8	17	16	49	77	94	82
9	13	11	77	48	yes	17
10	18	15	66	110	no	60

Unit 4 Subtraction: Subtracting from 10

	Set A	Set B	Set C	Set D	Set E	Set F
1	6	6	5	5	twice	6
2	1	3	3	2	5 times	3
3	3	9	1	8	10 times	2
4	7	5	2	1	2	7
5	9	10	1	3	4	8
6	2	7	1	8	no	7
7	4	4	2	10	5	2
8	10	2	7	3	10	3
9	5	8	1	4	2	6
10	8	1	3	yes	1	4

Answers

Unit 5 Subtraction: Subtracting 10, 9 or 11

	Set A	Set B	Set C	Set D	Set E	Set F
1	5	45	21	43	28	31
2	13	65	63	77	88	10
3	35	3	48	16	62	3
4	72	30	9	84	21	$23
5	88	69	16	29	38	26
6	27	42	73	62	12	17
7	38	38	69	34	43	87
8	80	29	17	22	83	74
9	11	8	62	20	54	11
10	64	71	79	31	78	9

Unit 6 Doubling and near doubling

	Set A	Set B	Set C	Set D	Set E	Set F
1	6	9	11	14	13	14
2	16	13	5	9	12	11
3	4	15	21	2	13	$24
4	18	3	9	4	18	18
5	0	7	15	16	4	11
6	14	11	19	3	3	16
7	2	1	13	12	2	12
8	10	19	7	5	22	6
9	12	17	17	4	4	9
10	8	5	3	10	6	8

Unit 7 Halving and near halving

	Set A	Set B	Set C	Set D	Set E	Set F
1	7	9	less	6	3	7
2	4	6	more	16	12	11
3	5	5	more	14	no	$10
4	1	4	less	4	11	6
5	9	12	more	18	yes	12
6	3	11	more	20	9	5
7	8	2	less	24	13	8
8	10	7	less	1	6	9
9	6	10	less	0	6	$2.10
10	2	3	less	8	10	4

Unit 8 Multiplication: The 2 times table

	Set A	Set B	Set C	Set D	Set E	Set F
1	yes	even	8	12	12	14
2	no	even	18	8	16	16
3	no	odd	10	4	9	10
4	yes	odd	14	10	no	6
5	no	odd	2	1	10	16
6	no	even	16	5	22	22
7	yes	odd	6	9	20	16
8	yes	even	22	0	24	$50
9	yes	even	20	11	6	40
10	yes	odd	0	7	16	8

Unit 9 Multiplication: The 3 times table

Set A	Set B	Set C	Set D	Set E	Set F
1 yes	1 no	1 9	1 3	1 21	1 12
2 no	2 no	2 24	2 4	2 27	2 4
3 yes	3 yes	3 33	3 9	3 15	3 33
4 yes	4 no	4 30	4 5	4 24	4 15
5 no	5 yes	5 18	5 11	5 33	5 21
6 no	6 yes	6 3	6 2	6 18	6 30
7 yes	7 no	7 36	7 6	7 0	7 9
8 no	8 yes	8 0	8 12	8 false	8 24
9 no	9 no	9 21	9 7	9 18	9 36
10 no	10 yes	10 15	10 1	10 60	10 27

Unit 10 Multiplication: The 4 times table

Set A	Set B	Set C	Set D	Set E	Set F
11	4	1 12	1 6	1 7	1 16
77	8	2 32	2 3	2 44	2 24
87	12	3 44	3 11	3 32	3 40
89	16	4 36	4 1	4 0	4 28
129	20	5 48	5 12	5 24	5 44
23	24	6 24	6 0	6 8	6 20
81	28	7 0	7 8	7 36	7 24
85	32	8 8	8 4	8 20	8 12
121	36	9 40	9 9	9 38	9 32
47	40	10 20	10 7	10 16	10 48

Unit 11 Multiplication: The 5 times and 10 times tables

Set A	Set B	Set C	Set D	Set E	Set F
11	1 2	1 3	1 20	1 30	1 40
23	2 1	2 7	2 60	2 100	2 100
48	3 3	3 5	3 40	3 55	3 15
93	4 4	4 8	4 120	4 100	4 80
772	5 3	5 6	5 25	5 40	5 35
27	6 1	6 9	6 40	6 40	6 90
81	7 4	7 3	7 45	7 3	7 35
64	8 3	8 6	8 110	8 70	8 70
89	9 1	9 1	9 35	9 100	9 $30
73	10 4	10 3	10 100	10 70	10 40

Unit 12 Division: Dividing by 2

Set A	Set B	Set C	Set D	Set E	Set F
6	1 7	1 6	1 true	1 10	1 7
22	2 11	2 14	2 true	2 7	2 50-cent
8	3 3	3 20	3 false	3 8	3 12
20	4 5	4 16	4 false	4 11	4 5
10	5 12	5 2	5 true	5 9	5 8
18	6 1	6 12	6 false	6 1	6 9
34	7 6	7 4	7 false	7 1	7 $6
56	8 2	8 10	8 true	8 yes	8 11
12	9 4	9 8	9 true	9 5	9 no
48	10 10	10 24	10 true	10 0	10 there is a remainder

Answers

Unit 13 Division: Dividing by 3

Set A	Set B	Set C	Set D	Set E	Set F
15	**1** 3	**1** 18	**1** 1	**1** 9	**1** 2
33	**2** 6	**2** 6	**2** 2	**2** 11	**2** 7
27	**3** 10	**3** 33	**3** 0	**3** 7	**3** 11
24	**4** 4	**4** 3	**4** 2	**4** 6	**4** 3
9	**5** 1	**5** 24	**5** 1	**5** 4	**5** $6
111	**6** 7	**6** 30	**6** 0	**6** 3	**6** 8
63	**7** 12	**7** 21	**7** 2	**7** 5	**7** 4
72	**8** 5	**8** 0	**8** 0	**8** 8	**8** 3
45	**9** 0	**9** 12	**9** 0	**9** 1	**9** 5
42	**10** 8	**10** 27	**10** 2	**10** 30	**10** 9

Unit 14 Division: Dividing by 4

Set A	Set B	Set C	Set D	Set E	Set F
31	**1** 7	**1** 20	**1** 3	**1** 11	**1** 2
77	**2** 10	**2** 36	**2** 3	**2** 8	**2** 6
69	**3** 2	**3** 12	**3** 2	**3** 6	**3** 4
121	**4** 3	**4** 0	**4** 2	**4** 4	**4** 3
235	**5** 5	**5** 44	**5** 3	**5** 1	**5** 12
23	**6** 1	**6** 8	**6** 2	**6** 16	**6** 9
37	**7** 4	**7** 40	**7** 3	**7** 10	**7** 10
19	**8** 6	**8** 28	**8** 3	**8** 36	**8** yes
251	**9** 9	**9** 24	**9** 2	**9** 18	**9** no
93	**10** 12	**10** 16	**10** 1	**10** 10	**10** 1

Unit 15 Division: Dividing by 5 and 10

Set A	Set B	Set C	Set D	Set E	Set F
23	**1** 3	**1** 3	**1** 30	**1** 7	**1** 7
92	**2** 4	**2** 11	**2** 70	**2** 6	**2** 5
789	**3** 1	**3** 6	**3** 100	**3** 4	**3** 8
57	**4** 0	**4** 0	**4** 20	**4** 7	**4** 10
79	**5** 1	**5** 5	**5** 80	**5** no	**5** $3
43	**6** 2	**6** 1	**6** 110	**6** 3	**6** 4
67	**7** 3	**7** 4	**7** 90	**7** yes	**7** 7
98	**8** 4	**8** 9	**8** 10	**8** 1	**8** 6
101	**9** 0	**9** 12	**9** 40	**9** 4	**9** 10
86	**10** 2	**10** 2	**10** 120	**10** 3	**10** 8

Unit 16 Fractions: Halves, quarters and parts of an amount

Set A	Set B	Set C	Set D	Set E	Set F
1 10	**1** 2	**1** 12	**1** 12	**1** 7	**1** 12
2 6	**2** 10	**2** 6	**2** 32	**2** 4	**2** 6
3 22	**3** 4	**3** 20	**3** 24	**3** 21	**3** 2
4 15	**4** 5	**4** 10	**4** 8	**4** 3	**4** 20
5 50	**5** 7	**5** 18	**5** 40	**5** $\frac{1}{4}$	**5** 22
6 9	**6** 20	**6** 4	**6** 36	**6** $\frac{1}{2}$	**6** $\frac{1}{2}$
7 30	**7** 8	**7** 22	**7** 20	**7** $\frac{1}{2}$	**7** $\frac{1}{4}$
8 44	**8** 9	**8** 8	**8** 44	**8** $\frac{1}{4}$	**8** 8
9 33	**9** 11	**9** 14	**9** 16	**9** no	**9** $\frac{1}{2}$
10 25	**10** 6	**10** 24	**10** 28	**10** yes	**10** $\frac{1}{4}$

Unit 17 Place value: Digit recognition

	Set A	Set B	Set C	Set D	Set E	Set F
1	U	68	374	120	90	10
2	H	28	921	340	160	10
3	T	33	357	770	30	300
4	T	48	313	820	8	1
5	U	79	273	900	34	30
6	H	82	312	325	870	10
7	T	90	163	488	440	300
8	U	500	780	215	no	2000
9	U	200	800	899	yes	$250
10	T	8	100	450	60	340

Unit 18 Rounding off: Nearest 10 and 100

	Set A	Set B	Set C	Set D	Set E	Set F
1	25	350	30	100	15	249
2	45	750	70	100	65	449
3	75	650	50	200	25	649
4	95	450	60	200	55	849
5	35	250	30	300	85	1049
6	15	550	120	800	105	1249
7	85	850	150	500	145	1549
8	125	950	140	900	245	1449
9	155	150	180	600	485	1349
10	195	1150	200	1000	545	2049

Unit 19 Sequences: Finding missing terms

	Set A	Set B	Set C	Set D	Set E	Set F
1	10	7	+4	14	50	–2
2	15	35	+5	20	30	–10
3	25	70	+10	80	20	–5
4	50	30	+3	40	16	–3
5	20	28	+2	15	24	–4
6	15	40	+5	68	58	–5
7	20	93	+10	78	57	–10
8	29	68	+4	34	19	–3
9	47	53	+3	29	68	–2
10	38	26	+2	45	19	–4

Unit 20 Number strings

	Set A	Set B	Set C	Set D	Set E	Set F
1	20	4	8	5	20	30 millimetres
2	20	4	12	10	21	$2
3	27	0	20	1	19	60
4	23	2	40	5	no	7
5	25	0	27	2	10	30
6	29	2	100	5	1	9
7	30	1	16	11	40	32
8	30	2	100	2	18	8
9	27	1	24	2	yes	8
10	37	0	32	3	3	13

Answers

Unit 21 Length: Units and conversions

	Set A	Set B	Set C	Set D	Set E	Set F
1	1	300	4	7000	5000	100
2	5	900	7	3000	3	9
3	8	400	3	8000	300	2
4	4	600	8	1000	8	400
5	9	1000	6	5000	8000	5
6	2	100	1	9000	2	1; 32
7	7	700	9	2000	500	800
8	10	200	5	4000	3	more
9	3	500	2	6000	800	no
10	6	800	10	10 000	600	220 cm

Unit 22 Perimeter: Concept and missing sides

	Set A	Set B	Set C	Set D	Set E	Set F
1	16 cm	7 cm	45 cm	9 cm	6 cm	11 metres
2	44 cm	10 cm	20 cm	3 cm	16 cm	300 metres
3	8 cm	2 cm	5 cm	6 cm	30 cm	false
4	28 cm	4 cm	30 cm	1 cm	20 cm	boundary
5	48 cm	8 cm	60 cm	12 cm	20 cm	23 cm
6	20 m	12 m	40 m	5 m	18 m	36 m
7	40 m	1 m	55 m	2 m	14 m	5
8	32 m	3 m	15 m	8 m	28 m	3 metres
9	24 m	9 m	20 m	11 m	24 m	30 metres
10	36 m	6 m	50 m	4 m	16 m	20 cm

Unit 23 Mass: Units and conversions

	Set A	Set B	Set C	Set D	Set E	Set F
1	4000 g	6 kg	grams	5 g	999 grams	2000
2	10 000 g	5 kg	grams	50 g	990 grams	500
3	7000 g	2 kg	kilograms	100 g	950 grams	200
4	6000 g	10 kg	grams	500 g	900 grams	2
5	3000 g	4 kg	kilograms	800 g	800 grams	more
6	5000 g	7 kg	kilograms	1000 g	500 grams	7000
7	9000 g	9 kg	grams	2 kg	100 grams	10
8	11 000 g	11 kg	kilograms	3 kg	50 grams	2
9	8000 g	3 kg	grams	5000 g	10 grams	5
10	1000 g	1 kg	kilograms	10 kg	1 gram	yes

Unit 24 Capacity/volume: Units and conversions

	Set A	Set B	Set C	Set D	Set E	Set F
1	9000 mL	7 L	millilitres	3 mL	999 mL	1000
2	10 000 mL	2 L	millilitres	30 mL	990 mL	500
3	5000 mL	11 L	litres	100 mL	950 mL	250
4	8000 mL	10 L	litres	300 mL	900 mL	5000
5	11 000 mL	3 L	millilitres	1000 mL	800 mL	3000
6	7000 mL	6 L	millilitres	2 L	500 mL	2000
7	4000 mL	9 L	millilitres	3000 mL	100 mL	5
8	3000 mL	5 L	millilitres	4 L	50 mL	4
9	6000 mL	4 L	litres	8000 mL	10 mL	4 glasses
10	1000 mL	1 L	litres	9 L	1 mL	10 box juices

Unit 25 Time: Positions of the hands

	Set A	Set B	Set C	Set D	Set E	Set F
1	4	20 past	3	7	5 minutes	8
2	2	20 to	8	8	35 minutes	12
3	3	25 past	5	8	20 minutes	10
4	5	5 to	10	7	55 minutes	10
5	1	5 past	6	7	25 minutes	11
6	10	10 past	11	7	15 minutes	12
7	7	25 to	1	8	45 minutes	15 minutes
8	11	10 to	4	8	10 minutes	12
9	9	15 past	9	8	30 minutes	5
10	8	15 to	2	7	40 minutes	3

Unit 26 Time: Digital and analogue conversions

	Set A	Set B	Set C	Set D	Set E	Set F
1	9:10	5 past 3	7:55	7:05	8:30	10 minutes
2	6:20	20 past 7	12:40	7:10	25 past 1	10 minutes
3	11:05	25 past 11	10:50	7:15	11:55	4:25
4	4:15	10 past 8	8:35	7:20	a quarter to 6	5 minutes
5	7:25	a quarter past 4	2:45	7:25	5:10	4:45
6	1:30	half past 1	5:50	7:30	10:15	5:45
7	8:10	20 past 12	8:45	8:00	8:10	15
8	12:20	a quarter past 2	6:35	8:10	25 to 4	20 minutes
9	5:15	5 past 6	11:40	8:25	10 to 10	25
10	3:05	25 past 9	4:55	8:30	3:35	20

Unit 27 Time: Unit equivalences

	Set A	Set B	Set C	Set D	Set E	Set F
1	60 seconds	7 days	summer	1 year	month	120 months
2	60 minutes	14 days	autumn	1 year	term	spring
3	600 seconds	70 days	autumn	1 week	seasons	autumn
4	600 minutes	28 days	autumn	1 month	30 seconds	fortnight
5	30 seconds	31 days	winter	1 semester	2	2
6	30 minutes	31 days	winter	1 fortnight	September	summer
7	120 seconds	31 days	winter	1 season	February	6 days
8	15 minutes	30 days	spring	1 minute	June	2 semesters
9	180 seconds	31 days	spring	1 hour	3 months	24
10	180 minutes	30 days	summer	winter	fortnight	520

Unit 28 Money: Note and coins

	Set A	Set B	Set C	Set D	Set E	Set F
1	20c	$10	2	1	$5 + 20c	60c
2	5c	$20	2	2	$5 + $1 + 50c	$3
3	50c	$100	3	2	$5 + $2	$20
4	$2	$5	3	2	$5 + $2 + $1 + 10c	85c
5	10c	$50	4	1	$5 + $2 + $2 + 50c	$3
6	50c	$100	2	2	$10 + $1	$3.85
7	$2	$5	3	2	$10 + $2 + 20c + 20c	50c and $1
8	50c	$100	2	4	$10 + $2 + $2	12
9	$1	$5	2	4	$10 + $5 + 50c	20
10	50c	$10	6	1	$10 + $5 + $2 + $1	10

Answers

Unit 29 Money: Amounts, and adding and giving change

	Set A	Set B	Set C	Set D	Set E	Set F
1	50c	$1	15c	1	$1	$1.50
2	80c	$1.50	40c	1	$2	2
3	90c	50c	35c	1	$2 + $1	90c
4	95c	10c	70c	2	$2 + 50c	3
5	10c	$1.90	80c	2	$2 + $2	45c
6	5c	$1.95	$2.50	1	$2 + $1 + 50c	3
7	20c	80c	$3.50	2	$2 + $1 + 50c + 20c + 10c	75c
8	75c	$1.10	$4.20	2	$2 + $2 + 50c	50c + 20c + 5c
9	85c	$1.80	$2.15	3	$2 + $2 + 50c + 20 c+ 10c	$4.90
10	70c	80c	$3.20	4	$2 + $2 + 50c + 20 c+ 20c + 5c	$2 + $2 + 50c + 20c + 20c

Unit 30 2D and 3D: Polygon and polyhedra properties

	Set A	Set B	Set C	Set D	Set E	Set F
1	1	6	Answers will vary.	square	rectangular prism	1 edge
2	4	6		rectangle	sphere	30 sides
3	4	5		square	cube	sphere
4	4	1		square	cylinder	rectangular prism
5	1	3		triangle	sphere	cylinder
6	5	2		triangle	rectangular prism	8
7	6	8		rectangle	triangular prism	triangle
8	8	5		circle	rectangular prism	hexagon
9	10	4		rectangle	cylinder	roof
10	3	7		circle	rectangular prism	rectangular prism

Unit 31 Chance: Concepts of likelihood

	Set A	Set B	Set C	Set D	Set E	Set F
1	possible	unlikely	$\frac{1}{6}$	1	$\frac{1}{10}$	certain
2	impossible	unlikely	$\frac{1}{6}$	3	$\frac{2}{10}$	possible
3	possible	unlikely	$\frac{2}{6}$	5	$\frac{1}{10}$	possible
4	impossible	likely	$\frac{2}{6}$	7	$\frac{2}{10}$	impossible
5	certain	unlikely	$\frac{2}{6}$	10	$\frac{5}{10}$	$\frac{1}{6}$
6	possible	likely	$\frac{3}{6}$	11	$\frac{5}{10}$	$\frac{1}{10}$
7	possible	likely	$\frac{3}{6}$	25	$\frac{4}{10}$	$\frac{1}{2}$
8	certain	unlikely	$\frac{4}{6}$	50	$\frac{6}{10}$	impossible
9	impossible	likely	$\frac{5}{6}$	100	$\frac{9}{10}$	certain
10	impossible	likely	$\frac{5}{6}$	500	$\frac{9}{10}$	$\frac{0}{6}$

Unit 32 Revision: All sorts

	Set A	Set B	Set C	Set D	Set E	Set F
1	6	14	11	400 cm	10	13
2	27	24	4	8 m	25c	14
3	19	28	300	16 cm	20	5
4	36	35	30	2000	6	Thursday
5	3	90	11	7 kg	30	4
6	35	12	16	4000 mL	impossible	pentagons
7	45	4	16	5 past 11	impossible	300
8	25	11	36	30 days	certain	20
9	26	12	5	8	certain	100
10	23	8	1	3	possible	8

Set C

Divide these numbers by 5:

1	15	
2	55	
3	30	
4	0	
5	25	
6	5	
7	20	
8	45	
9	60	
10	10	

Set D

Which numbers have been divided by 10 to produce the following answers?

1	3	
2	7	
3	10	
4	2	
5	8	
6	11	
7	9	
8	1	
9	4	
10	12	

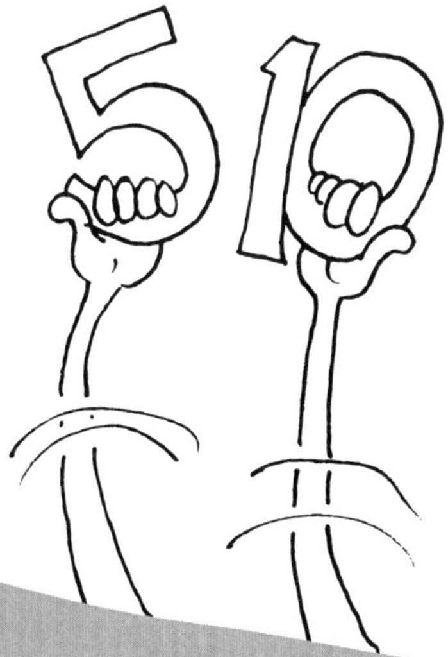

Set F

1 My set of pentagons has 35 sides. I have ____ pentagons in my set.

2 In my piggy bank I have $25, all in $5 notes. In my piggy bank are ____ five dollar notes.

3 I have 40 cents in 5 cent coins. I have ____ 5 cent coins.

4 The pentathlon is an event with 5 different sports in it. I completed 50 pentathlon sports last summer. Last summer I participated in ____ pentathlons.

5 I shared $15 with 4 of my friends. We each received $____.

6 Our school owns some mini buses, which each hold 10 children. 40 children were on an excursion yesterday and were in ____ mini buses.

7 Scorpions have10 legs. My friend Boris has a collection of pet scorpions which, altogether, have 70 legs. Boris owns ____ pet scorpions.

8 My family can boast a total of 60 fingers among them. There are ____ people in my family.

9 My great-great-grandmother is 100 years old. She has lived for ____ decades.

10 The 80 children in Grade 3 were divided into 10 teams for house sport. There were ____ children in each team.

Number and Algebra

Unit 16 Fractions: Halves, quarters and parts of an amount

A fraction is a piece or a part of a larger thing or group. Fractions are very similar to division sums. Finding a half of something is the same as dividing it by 2. Finding a quarter of something is the same as dividing it by 4, and so on.

Set A

1 $\frac{1}{2}$ of 20 = ☐
2 $\frac{1}{2}$ of 12 = ☐
3 $\frac{1}{2}$ of 44 = ☐
4 $\frac{1}{2}$ of 30 = ☐
5 $\frac{1}{2}$ of 100 = ☐
6 $\frac{1}{2}$ of 18 = ☐
7 $\frac{1}{2}$ of 60 = ☐
8 $\frac{1}{2}$ of 88 = ☐
9 $\frac{1}{2}$ of 66 = ☐
10 $\frac{1}{2}$ of 50 = ☐

Set B

1 $\frac{1}{4}$ of 8 = ☐
2 $\frac{1}{4}$ of 40 = ☐
3 $\frac{1}{4}$ of 16 = ☐
4 $\frac{1}{4}$ of 20 = ☐
5 $\frac{1}{4}$ of 28 = ☐
6 $\frac{1}{4}$ of 80 = ☐
7 $\frac{1}{4}$ of 32 = ☐
8 $\frac{1}{4}$ of 36 = ☐
9 $\frac{1}{4}$ of 44 = ☐
10 $\frac{1}{4}$ of 24 = ☐

Set E

1 Find a half of 14 ____
2 Find a quarter of 16 ____
3 Split 42 into 2 equal pieces ____
4 Split 12 into 4 equal pieces ____
5 What fraction of 40 is 10? ____
6 What fraction of 40 is 20? ____
7 What fraction of 32 is 16? ____
8 What fraction of 80 is 20? ____
9 Is 23 a half of 66? ____
10 Is 15 a quarter of 60? ____

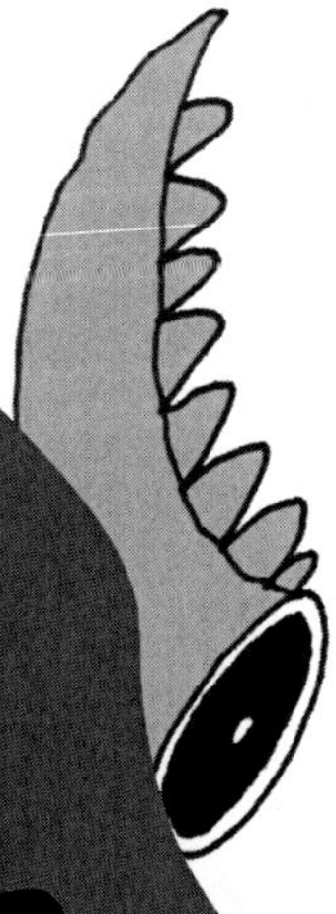

Set C

How many halves are in the following number of soccer games?

1	6	
2	3	
3	10	
4	5	
5	9	
6	2	
7	11	
8	4	
9	7	
10	12	

Set D

How many quarters are in the following number of basketball games?

1	3	
2	8	
3	6	
4	2	
5	10	
6	9	
7	5	
8	11	
9	4	
10	7	

Set F

1 Half of my 24 stickers are swaps. I have ____ swaps.

2 A quarter of 24 tomatoes are damaged. ____ tomatoes are damaged.

3 There are ____ quarters in half a game of football.

4 5 games of basketball contain ____ quarters.

5 11 games of hockey contain ____ halves.

6 3 months is ____ of a semester.

7 If there are 4 terms in a school year, each term is ____ of the year.

8 My glass holds $\frac{1}{4}$ of a litre of milk. ____ of these glasses will come from a 2 litre bottle of milk.

9 6 months is what fraction of a year? ____

10 3 months is what fraction of a year? ____

NSW: Number concepts NS2.4; Qld: Number concepts N3.1;
Vic: Numbers, counting and numeration 3.3; WA: Number N3.1b; SA: Number 2.6

Number and Algebra

Unit 17
Place Value: Digit recognition

We all know that our counting or numeration system is based on the number 10, because we have 10 fingers. So, each time we have 10 of a basic unit, we need to introduce a new value. 10 ones or units make a 10; 10 tens make a hundred; 10 hundreds make a thousand, and so on.

Set A

What is the 3 worth in the following numbers? Write 'U' for units, 'T' for tens and 'H' for hundreds.

1 23 ☐
2 358 ☐
3 732 ☐
4 837 ☐
5 403 ☐
6 396 ☐
7 830 ☐
8 943 ☐
9 103 ☐
10 731 ☐

Set B

Write down the values of these numbers:

1 **6 tens + 8 units** ☐
2 **2 tens + 8 units** ☐
3 **3 tens + 3 units** ☐
4 **5 tens - 2 units** ☐
5 **8 tens - 1 unit** ☐
6 **9 tens - 8 units** ☐
7 **3 tens x 3 =** ☐
8 **5 tens x 10 =** ☐
9 **4 tens x 5 =** ☐
10 **8 tens divided by 10 =** ☐

Set E

1 Find the total when 4 tens are added to 5 tens ___
2 Find the product of 8 tens and 2 ___
3 Find the difference between 6 tens and 3 tens ___
4 Find the quotient of 8 tens and 10 ___
5 How many tens make 340? ___
6 How many units make 87 tens? ___
7 How many units make 4 hundreds plus 4 tens? ___
8 Do 20 tens equal two thousand? ___
9 Do 30 tens equal 300? ___
10 By how much are 10 tens bigger than 4 tens? ___

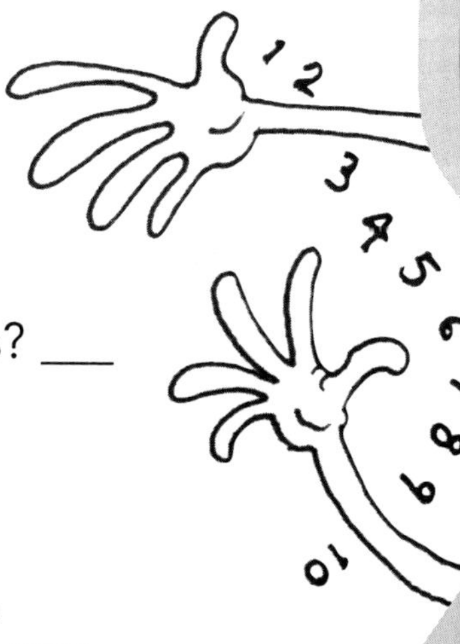

Set C

What do these numbers combine to make?

1. 3 hundreds + 7 tens + 4 units
2. 9 hundreds + 2 tens + 1 unit
3. 5 tens + 3 hundreds + 7 units
4. 3 units + 3 hundreds + 1 ten
5. 3 units + 7 tens + 2 hundreds
6. 3 hundreds + 2 units + 1 ten
7. 6 tens + 3 units + 1 hundred
8. 8 hundreds – 2 tens
9. 2 hundreds x 4 =
10. (4 tens + 5 tens) + 10

Set D

What is the value of these numbers?

1. 12 tens
2. 34 tens
3. 77 tens
4. 82 tens
5. 90 tens
6. 32 tens + 5
7. 48 tens + 8
8. 22 tens – 5
9. 90 tens – 1
10. 40 tens + 5 tens

Set F

1. How many 10-cent coins will I need to make $1? ____
2. How many $10 notes will I need to make $100? ____
3. How many $1 coins will I need to make $300? _____
4. How many $100 notes will I need to make $100? ____
5. How many decades make 300 years? ____
6. How many centuries make a thousand years?____
7. How many centimetres make 3 metres? _____
8. How many metres make 2 kilometres? ______
9. How much money would you have if you had five $10 notes and two $100 notes? ______
10. How many cents would you have if you had three $1 coins and four 10 cent coins? _____

Number and Algebra

Unit 18
Rounding off: Nearest 10 and 100

When numbers are rounded off, they are taken to the nearest 10 or to the nearest 100, depending on the question that has been asked. If a number is exactly halfway, it is taken up and not down. So 25 to the nearest 10 would equal 30; 650 to the nearest 100 would equal 700, and so on.

Set A

What number is halfway between:

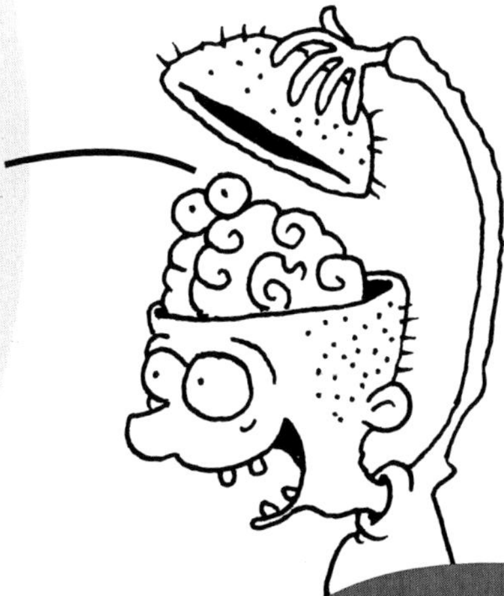

1 20 and 30 ☐
2 40 and 50 ☐
3 70 and 80 ☐
4 90 and 100 ☐
5 30 and 40 ☐
6 10 and 20 ☐
7 80 and 90 ☐
8 120 and 130 ☐
9 150 and 160 ☐
10 190 and 200 ☐

Set B

What number is halfway between:

1 300 and 400 ☐
2 700 and 800 ☐
3 600 and 700 ☐
4 400 and 500 ☐
5 200 and 300 ☐
6 500 and 600 ☐
7 800 and 900 ☐
8 900 and 1000 ☐
9 100 and 200 ☐
10 1100 and 1200 ☐

Set C

Round these numbers to the nearest 10:

1	34	
2	67	
3	49	
4	55	
5	26	
6	123	
7	145	
8	137	
9	183	
10	195	

Set D

Round these numbers to the nearest 100:

1	142	
2	149	
3	150	
4	237	
5	271	
6	750	
7	480	
8	881	
9	619	
10	951	

Set E

What is the smallest number that, when rounded to the nearest 10, will equal:

1	20	
2	70	
3	30	
4	60	
5	90	
6	110	
7	150	
8	250	
9	490	
10	550	

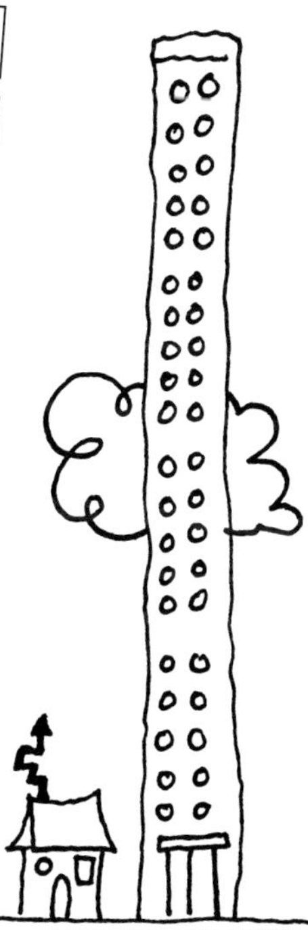

Set F

What is the biggest number that, when rounded to the nearest 100, will equal:

1	200	
2	400	
3	600	
4	800	
5	1000	
6	1200	
7	1500	
8	1400	
9	1300	
10	2000	

Number and Algebra

Unit 19 Sequences: Finding missing terms

A sequence is a pattern usually including numbers, but sometimes letters, or even symbols. Each member of a sequence is called a term and each sequence's pattern is called a rule. So, the sequence 2, 4, 6, 8, ... has 6 as its 3rd term, and the rule of +2 (or the 2 times table, or even numbers).

Find the next term in these sequences:

Set A

1 2, 4 ,6, 8, ____

2 3, 6, 9, 12, ____

3 5, 10, 15, 20, ____

4 10, 20, 30, 40, ____

5 4, 8, 12, 16, ____

6 7, 9, 11, 13, ____

7 8, 11, 14, 17, ____

8 9, 14, 19, 24, ____

9 7, 17, 27, 37, ____

10 22, 26, 30, 34, ____

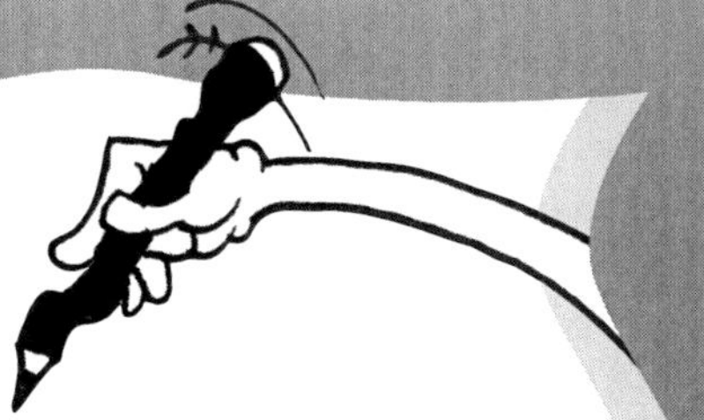

Set B

What is the missing term in these sequences?

1 1, 3, 5, ____, 9

2 20, 25, 30, ____, 40

3 40, 50, 60, ____, 80

4 21, 24, 27,____, 33

5 16, 20, 24, ____, 32

6 34, 36, 38, ____, 42

7 78, 83, 88, ____, 98

8 38, 48, 58, ____,78

9 41, 45, 49, ____, 57

10 17, 20, 23,____, 29

Set C

What are the rules of these sequences?

1 4, 8, 12, 16, ... ______

2 45, 50, 55, ... ______

3 50, 60, 70, ... ______

4 9, 12, 15, ... ______

5 18, 20, 22, ... ______

6 7, 12, 17, ... ______

7 33, 43 ,53, ... ______

8 15, 19, 23, ... ______

9 26, 29, 32, ... ______

10 87, 89, 91, ... ______

Set D

Find the next term in these sequences:

1 22, 20, 18, 16, ____

2 36, 32, 28, 24, ____

3 120, 110, 100, 90, ____

4 60, 55, 50, 45, ____

5 27, 24, 21, 18, ____

6 80, 77, 74, 71, ____

7 98, 93, 88, 83, ____

8 74, 64, 54, 44, ____

9 45, 41, 37, 33, ____

10 53, 51, 49, 47, ____

Set E

Find the missing terms in these sequences:

1 30, 40, ____, 60, 70

2 45, 40, 35, ____, 25

3 28, 24, ____, 16, 12

4 22, 20, 18, ____, 14

5 27, ____, 21, 18, 15

6 78, 68, ____, 48, 38

7 61, 59, ____, 55, 53

8 27, 23, ____, 15, 11

9 77, 74, 71, ____, 65

10 34, 29, 24, ____, 14

Set F

What are the rules of these sequences?

1 22, 20, 18, 16, ... ____

2 90, 80, 70, 60, ... ____

3 45, 40, 35, 30, ... ____

4 21, 18, 15, 12, ... ____

5 36, 32, 28, 24, ... ____

6 73, 68, 63, 58, ... ____

7 93, 83, 73, 63, ... ____

8 31, 28, 25, 22, ... ____

9 19, 17, 15, 13, ... ____

10 51, 47, 43, 39, ... ____

Number and Algebra

Unit 20 Number Strings

Number strings are lots of mini questions tied together to make a longer question. Work left to right to try and solve these tricky problems.

Set A

1 5 + 5 + 5 + 5 =

2 9 + 7 + 3 + 1 =

3 8 + 6 + 4 + 2 + 7 =

4 9 + 4 + 6 + 3 + 1 =

5 3 + 9 + 7 + 5 + 1 =

6 8 + 9 + 4 + 6 + 2 =

7 6 + 4 + 7 + 3 + 9 + 1 =

8 4 + 6 + 9 + 1 + 2 + 8 =

9 5 + 6 + 4 + 7 + 5 =

10 10 + 8 + 10 + 2 + 7 =

Set B

1 10 - 2 - 2 - 2 =

2 9 - 1 - 1 - 3 =

3 8 - 1 - 3 - 4 =

4 10 - 5 - 2 - 1 =

5 8 - 6 - 1 - 1 =

6 6 - 1 - 1 - 2 =

7 9 - 6 - 1 - 1 =

8 10 - 3 - 3 - 2 =

9 10 - 2 - 3 - 4 =

10 7 - 5 - 1 - 1 =

Set E

1 What is the sum of 4 and 6 and 9 and 1? ____

2 Find the total of 10 and 3 and 8 ____

3 What is 2 and 8 and 4 and 5 altogether? ____

4 Is 6 and 7 and 3 and 2 bigger than 20? ____

5 Take 3 and 7 and 5 and 5 away from 30 ____

6 What is the difference between 5 plus 5 and 3 plus 6? ____

7 Find the product of 2 and 5 and 2 and 2 ____

8 What is the answer to 3 multiplied by itself and then doubled? ____

9 Divide 20 by 2 and by 2 again. Is the answer 5? ____

10 Find the quotient of 30 and 5 and then divide this by 2 ____

Set C

1 $2 \times 2 \times 2 =$ ☐

2 $3 \times 2 \times 2 =$ ☐

3 $5 \times 2 \times 2 =$ ☐

4 $10 \times 2 \times 2 =$ ☐

5 $3 \times 3 \times 3 =$ ☐

6 $10 \times 5 \times 2 =$ ☐

7 $4 \times 2 \times 2 =$ ☐

8 $5 \times 10 \times 2 =$ ☐

9 $2 \times 3 \times 4 =$ ☐

10 $4 \times 2 \times 1 \times 2 \times 2 =$ ☐

Set D

1 $20 \div 2 \div 2 =$ ☐

2 $20 \div 2 \div 1 =$ ☐

3 $25 \div 5 \div 5 =$ ☐

4 $10 \div 2 \div 1 =$ ☐

5 $40 \div 5 \div 4 =$ ☐

6 $50 \div 10 \div 1 =$ ☐

7 $55 \div 5 \div 1 =$ ☐

8 $60 \div 10 \div 3 =$ ☐

9 $24 \div 3 \div 4 =$ ☐

10 $45 \div 5 \div 3 =$ ☐

Set F

1 Here are the rainfall totals for this week in millimetres: Monday 6, Tuesday 9, Wednesday 4, Thursday 1 and Friday 10. How much rain fell this week? ___________

2 I had $10 in my purse and spent $5 then $2 then $1. I then had $____ left.

3 In Aussie Rules, 6 points equals a goal. I kicked 5 goals last week and 5 goals this week. Altogether, my goals were worth ____ points for my team.

4 I gave half of my 24 stickers to Jessie and 5 more to Sam. I was left with ____ stickers.

5 Slugger Smedley is a fine batsman. He scored 4, 4, 4, 6, 6 and 6. He scored ____ runs altogether.

6 There are 20 children in my class but 5 are ill, 2 are at Music and 4 are on yard duty. At the moment, there are ____ children in the class.

7 My little sister is 4. I am twice as old as her, my big brother is twice as old as me, and my uncle is twice as old as my big brother. My uncle is ____ years old.

8 Mum cut my birthday cake in half, in half again and in half again. How many pieces of cake are there now? ____

9 My pet rabbit weighed 1 kilogram then doubled in size and doubled in size and doubled in size again. He now weighs ____ kilograms.

10 My 24 baby teeth are being replaced quickly. I lost 7 last year and 4 this year so far. How many baby teeth do I have left? ____

Measurement and Geometry

Unit 21 Length: Units and Conversions

Remember that there are 100 centimetres in a metre and 1000 metres in a kilometre.

Set A

1 100 cm = ☐ m
2 500 cm = ☐ m
3 800 cm = ☐ m
4 400 cm = ☐ m
5 900 cm = ☐ m
6 200 cm = ☐ m
7 700 cm = ☐ m
8 1000 cm = ☐ m
9 300 cm = ☐ m
10 600 cm = ☐ m

Set B

1 3 m = ☐ cm
2 9 m = ☐ cm
3 4 m = ☐ cm
4 6 m = ☐ cm
5 10 m = ☐ cm
6 1 m = ☐ cm
7 7 m = ☐ cm
8 2 m = ☐ cm
9 5 m = ☐ cm
10 8 m = ☐ cm

Set E

1 How many metres in 5 kilometres? ______
2 How many kilometres equal 3000 metres? ______
3 3 metres is the same as ______ centimetres.
4 800 centimetres is the same as ______ metres.
5 How many metres in 8 kilometres? ______
6 How many kilometres equal 2000 metres? ______
7 5 metres is the same as ______ centimetres.
8 300 centimetres is the same as ______ metres.
9 5 metres and 3 metres equals ______ centimetres.
10 Take away 2 metres from 8 metres.
This leaves ______ centimetres.

Set C

1 4000 m = ☐ km
2 7000 m = ☐ km
3 3000 m = ☐ km
4 8000 m = ☐ km
5 6000 m = ☐ km
6 1000 m = ☐ km
7 9000 m = ☐ km
8 5000 m = ☐ km
9 2000 m = ☐ km
10 10 000 m = ☐ km

Set D

1 7 km = ☐ m
2 3 km = ☐ m
3 8 km = ☐ m
4 1 km = ☐ m
5 5 km = ☐ m
6 9 km = ☐ m
7 2 km = ☐ m
8 4 km = ☐ m
9 6 km = ☐ m
10 10 km = ☐ m

Set F

1 I jumped 3 metres. Sam jumped 4 metres. He jumped ______ centimetres more than me.

2 The world's long-jump record is 895 centimetres. This is about ______ metres.

3 High jumpers can clear over 200 centimetres. This is over ______ metres.

4 My bedroom is 4 metres long. This is ______ centimetres long.

5 My dog is 95 centimetres tall. He is ______ centimetres shorter than 1 metre.

6 My brother is 132 centimetres tall. He is ______ metres and ______ centimetres tall.

7 Dad's tape measure is 8 metres long. It can measure up to ______ centimetres in length.

8 Our local pool is 20 metres long. Is this more or less than 200 centimetres in length? ______

9 This pool is 1200 centimetres in width. Is this more than 120 metres in width? ______

10 Would this pool be 220 metres or 220 centimetres deep? ______

Measurement and Geometry

Unit 22
Perimeter: Concept and missing sides

The perimeter of a shape is the distance around its boundary or the sum of the lengths of its sides.

Set A

Find the perimeters of squares with side lengths of:

1	4 cm	
2	11 cm	
3	2 cm	
4	7 cm	
5	12 cm	
6	5 m	
7	10 m	
8	8 m	
9	6 m	
10	9 m	

Set B

What would the side lengths of a square be, if its perimeter was:

1	28 cm	
2	40 cm	
3	8 cm	
4	16 cm	
5	32 cm	
6	48 m	
7	4 m	
8	12 m	
9	36 m	
10	24 m	

Set E

Find the perimeters of these rectangles, given the following lengths (L) and widths (W):

1 L = 2 cm, W = 1 cm _____

2 L = 5 cm, W = 3 cm _____

3 L = 10 cm, W = 5 cm _____

4 L = 8 cm, W = 2 cm _____

5 L = 7 cm, W = 3 cm _____

6 L = 5 m, W = 4 m _____

7 L = 4 m, W = 3 m _____

8 L = 8 m, W = 6 m _____

9 L= 7 m, W = 5 m _____

10 L = 6 m, W = 2 m _____

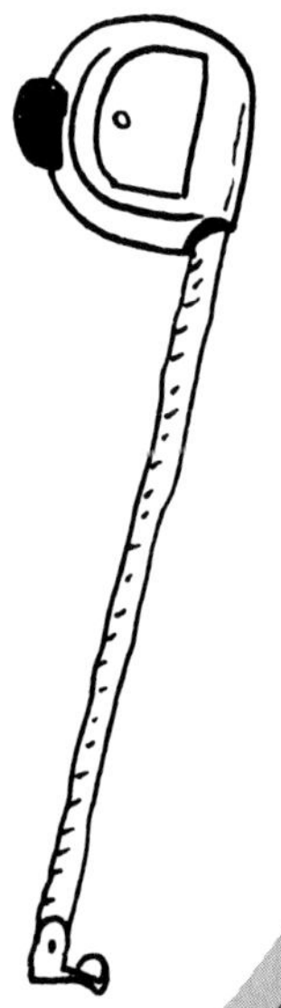

Set C

Find the perimeter of a regular pentagon with side lengths of:

1. **9 cm** ☐
2. **4 cm** ☐
3. **1 cm** ☐
4. **6 cm** ☐
5. **12 cm** ☐
6. **8 m** ☐
7. **11 m** ☐
8. **3 m** ☐
9. **4 m** ☐
10. **10 m** ☐

Set D

What would the side lengths of a regular pentagon be, if its perimeter was:

1. **45 cm** ☐
2. **15 cm** ☐
3. **30 cm** ☐
4. **5 cm** ☐
5. **60 cm** ☐
6. **25 m** ☐
7. **10 m** ☐
8. **40 m** ☐
9. **55 m** ☐
10. **20 m** ☐

Set F

1 A square has a perimeter of 44 metres. Its side lengths must be ________.

2 A paddock is 100 metres long and 50 metres wide. Its perimeter is ________.

3 Perimeter is measured in square units. True or false? ________.

4 Find a word starting with 'bou' that means the same as perimeter ________.

5 Find the perimeter of a triangle with side lengths of 4 cm, 8 cm and 11 cm.

______

6 An equilateral triangle has 3 equal side lengths. Find the perimeter of such a triangle with side lengths of 12 m. ______

7 To find the perimeter of a regular pentagon, measure 1 side and then multiply by _____.

8 A regular pentagon has a perimeter of 15 metres. Its side lengths are ________.

9 Would the perimeter of a classroom be 30 metres or 30 square metres? ________.

10 There are 2 squares. 1 has side lengths of 5 cm, the other side lengths of 10 cm. Find the difference in the perimeters of the 2 squares.______

Measurement and Geometry

Unit 23
Mass: Units and conversions

Remember that all weights are based on the gram and that 1000 grams equals 1 kilogram.

Set A

How many grams equal:

1	4 kg	
2	10 kg	
3	7 kg	
4	6 kg	
5	3 kg	
6	5 kg	
7	9 kg	
8	11 kg	
9	8 kg	
10	1 kg	

Set B

Change these into kilograms:

1	6000 g	
2	5000 g	
3	2000 g	
4	10 000 g	
5	4000 g	
6	7000 g	
7	9000 g	
8	11 000 g	
9	3000 g	
10	1000 g	

Set E

How far from a kilogram are the following masses?

1 1 gram ______
2 10 grams ______
3 50 grams ______
4 100 grams ______
5 200 grams ______
6 500 grams ______
7 900 grams ______
8 950 grams ______
9 990 grams ______
10 999 grams ______

Set C

Would it be more sensible to measure the mass of these items in grams or kilograms?

1 **an apple** ____________
2 **a ball** ____________
3 **a brick** ____________
4 **a block of butter** ____________
5 **a dog** ____________
6 **a length of timber** ____________
7 **an onion** ____________
8 **my sister** ____________
9 **a doll** ____________
10 **a car tyre** ____________

Set D

Put the following masses in order from lightest to heaviest:

50 g 10 kg 800 g 1000 g 3 kg
500 g 5000 g 5 g 100 g 2 kg

Lightest 1 __________
2 __________
3 __________
4 __________
5 __________
6 __________
7 __________
8 __________
9 __________
Heaviest 10 __________

Set F

1 This year I have put on 2 kilograms in weight. This is equal to ______ grams.

2 My pair of school shoes weighs 1 kilogram. Each shoe weighs _____ grams.

3 My drink bottle, when filled, weighs 800 grams. This is _____ grams away from a kilogram.

4 My rabbit, Monty, weighs 2000 grams. This equals ____ kilograms.

5 Monty's food comes in a box weighing 1200 grams. Is this more or less than a kilogram? _______

6 Monty's cage weighs 7 kilograms. This equals _______ grams.

7 Monty eats 100 grams of carrot a day. In ____ days he will eat a kilogram of carrots.

8 A can of cherries weighs 500 grams. ____ cans will weigh a kilogram.

9 A banana weighs 200 grams. ____ bananas will weigh a kilogram.

10 If you eat 200 grams of fibre a day, will you eat a kilogram of fibre in a week? _____

Measurement and Geometry

Unit 24
Capacity/volume: Units and conversions

Remember that all capacities are based on the litre and that 1000 millilitres equals 1 litre.

Set A

How many millilitres equal:

1	9 litres	
2	10 litres	
3	5 litres	
4	8 litres	
5	11 litres	
6	7 litres	
7	4 litres	
8	3 litres	
9	6 litres	
10	1 litre	

Set B

Change these into litres:

1	7000 mL	
2	2000 mL	
3	11 000 mL	
4	10 000 mL	
5	3000 mL	
6	6000 mL	
7	9000 mL	
8	5000 mL	
9	4000 mL	
10	1000 mL	

Set E

How far from a litre are the following measures?

1 1 millilitre ________

2 10 millilitres ________

3 50 millilitres ________

4 100 millilitres ________

5 200 millilitres ________

6 500 millilitres ________

7 900 millilitres ________

8 950 millilitres ________

9 990 millilitres ________

10 999 millilitres ________

Set C

Would it be more sensible to measure the volume of these items in millilitres or litres?

1 **a box juice** __________

2 **a glass** __________

3 **a barrel** __________

4 **a petrol tank** __________

5 **a can of soup** __________

6 **a water bottle** __________

7 **a carton of cream** __________

8 **a shampoo bottle** __________

9 **a water tank** __________

10 **an orange juice carton** __________

Set D

Put the following volumes in order from least to greatest:

30 mL 9 L 8000 mL 1000 mL 4 L
300 mL 3000 mL 3 mL 100 mL 2L

Least 1 ________

2 ________

3 ________

4 ________

5 ________

6 ________

7 ________

8 ________

9 ________

Greatest 10 ________

Set F

1 I used 1 litre of water to mix my playdough. This is equal to ______ millilitres of water.

2 My school drink bottle holds 500 millilitres. This is _____ millilitres short of a litre.

3 In my fridge is a 1250 millilitre bottle of cola. This is equal to 1 litre and _____ millilitres.

4 My bathroom sink holds 5 litres of water. This is equal to ______ millilitres.

5 This sink is currently filled up to 2 litres from the top. It now contains ______ millilitres of water.

6 How many more millilitres of water could I pour into this sink before it overflowed? ____

7 Our soup bowls hold 200 millilitres. How many bowls could I fill from a 1 litre can of soup? ____

8 How many 300 millilitre bottles of cream will be needed for a recipe requiring 1 litre of cream?____

9 A drinking glass holds 250 millilitres. How many glasses could be filled from a litre bottle of cola? _____

10 How many 100 millilitre box juices will be needed to fill a 1 litre drink bottle? _____

Measurement and Geometry

Unit 25
Time: Positions of the hands

Remember that the long hand measures the minutes on a clock face and that each of the 12 numbers represents 5-minute intervals. Also remember that the short hand measures the hours.

Set A

To which number does the big hand point when the time is:

1 20 past
2 10 past
3 a quarter past
4 25 past
5 5 past
6 10 minutes to
7 25 to
8 5 to
9 a quarter to
10 20 to

Set B

How many minutes to or past the hour will it be when the big hand is pointing to the:

1 4
2 8
3 5
4 11
5 1
6 2
7 7
8 10
9 3
10 9

Set E

How many minutes away from the next hour will the time be if the big hand is on the:

1 11 ______
2 5 ______
3 8 ______
4 1 ______
5 7 ______
6 9 ______
7 3 ______
8 10 ______
9 6 ______
10 4 ______

Set C

To which number would the big hand point at:

1	**8:15**	
2	**8:40**	
3	**8:25**	
4	**8:50**	
5	**8:30**	
6	**8:55**	
7	**8:05**	
8	**8:20**	
9	**8:45**	
10	**8:10**	

Set D

Would the hour hand be closer to the 7 or closer to the 8 when the time is:

1	**7:10**	
2	**7:40**	
3	**7:55**	
4	**7:05**	
5	**7:25**	
6	**7:15**	
7	**7:35**	
8	**7:50**	
9	**7:45**	
10	**7:20**	

Set F

1 Our school day starts at 8:40, when the big hand is on the _____.

2 First lesson starts at 9 o'clock when the big hand is on the _____.

3 Art starts at 9:50 when the big hand is on the _____.

4 Art starts when the little hand is closest to the _____.

5 Recess starts at 10:30 and goes for 25 minutes. At the end of recess the minute hand is on the_____.

6 Music starts at 12:00. At 12:00 the 2 hands are on the _____.

7 Lunch finishes when the hour hand is near the 2 and the minute hand is on the 9. How far away from 2 o'clock is this? _____________

8 PE lasts for 30 minutes and starts at 2:30. At the end of PE the minute hand is on the _____.

9 The last bell for the school day rings at 3:25. At this time, the big hand is on the _____.

10 I get home after school at 4:15. At this time the minute hand is on the ______.

Measurement and Geometry

Unit 26
Time: Digital and analogue conversions

Remember that an analogue or sweep-hand clock tells the time in minutes to or from the hour. A digital clock tells the time just in numbers.

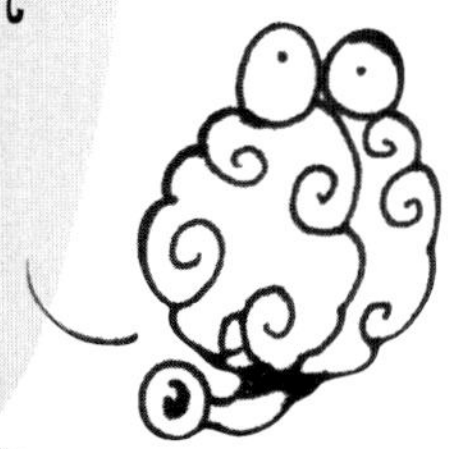

Set A

Change these sweep-hand times into digital times:

1 10 past 9 ____
2 20 past 6 ____
3 5 past 11 ____
4 a quarter past 4 ____
5 25 past 7 ____
6 half past 1 ____
7 10 past 8 ____
8 20 past 12 ____
9 a quarter past 5 ____
10 5 past 3 ____

Set B

Change these digital times into analogue times:

1 3:05 ____________
2 7:20 ____________
3 11:25 ____________
4 8:10 ____________
5 4:15 ____________
6 1:30 ____________
7 12:20 ____________
8 2:15 ____________
9 6:05 ____________
10 9:25 ____________

Set E

Which time comes first?

1 20 to 9 or 8:30 __________
2 1:30 or 25 past 1 __________
3 11:55 or 12:05 __________
4 a quarter to 6 or a quarter past 6 __________
5 5:10 or 10:05 __________
6 10:15 or half past 10 __________
7 8:10 or 20 past 8 __________
8 4:40 or 25 to 4 __________
9 9:55 or 10 to 10 __________
10 3:35 or 20 to 4 __________

Set C

Change these sweep-hand times into digital times:

1 **5 to 8** ______

2 **20 to 1** ______

3 **10 to 11** ______

4 **25 to 9** ______

5 **a quarter to 3** ______

6 **10 to 6** ______

7 **a quarter to 9** ______

8 **25 to 7** ______

9 **20 to 12** ______

10 **5 to 5** ______

Set D

Put these times in order. Answer in digital time:

a quarter past 7 8 o'clock half past 7 25 past 7

8:30 7:10 8:25 20 past 7 7:05 8:10

Earliest time 1 ________

2 ________

3 ________

4 ________

5 ________

6 ________

7 ________

8 ________

9 ________

Latest time 10 ________

Set F

1 My footy match started at 2:50. How far away from 3 o'clock is this? __________

2 The footy match ended at 4:10. How long after 4 o'clock is this? __________

3 I left the ground a quarter of an hour after the match. I left at ______.

4 How far away from 4:30 did I leave the ground? __________

5 I get home from the game at a quarter to 5. What did my digital clock look like at this time? ______

6 My favourite TV show starts at 5:15 and runs for 30 minutes. It ends at ______

7 Dinner usually starts at 5:55 and finishes at 10 past 6. Dinner takes ______ minutes to eat.

8 At 7 o'clock I like to read for about 40 minutes. How far from 8 o'clock do I stop reading? __________

9 At 8 o'clock I get ready for bed and I am usually asleep by 8:35. This is ______ minutes from 9 o'clock.

10 I normally wake up at about 7:40. This can be said to be ______ minutes to 8 o'clock.

Measurement and Geometry

Unit 27
Time: Unit equivalences

These questions deal with the way the year is divided up into many different units such as second, minute, hour, day, week, fortnight, month, term, season, semester and year. Do you know all of these units?

Set A

Change each minute into seconds and each hour into minutes:

1 **1 minute** ____________
2 **1 hour** ____________
3 **10 minutes** ____________
4 **10 hours** ____________
5 **half a minute** ____________
6 **half an hour** ____________
7 **2 minutes** ____________
8 **a quarter of an hour** ____________
9 **3 minutes** ____________
10 **3 hours** ____________

Set B

Change into days:

1 **1 week** _______
2 **1 fortnight** _______
3 **10 weeks** _______
4 **2 fortnights** _______
5 **May** _______
6 **January** _______
7 **December** _______
8 **April** _______
9 **March** _______
10 **September** _______

Set E

1 What do we have 12 times a year? __________
2 What occurs 4 times a year at school? __________
3 The year is split up into 4 __________, each lasting 3 months.
4 Half a minute lasts for how many seconds? _____________
5 A fortnight equals _____weeks.
6 Spring starts with the month of_____________.
7 Summer ends in the month of _____________.
8 Winter begins in _____________.
9 Autumn lasts for _____ months.
10 A __________ is longer than a week but shorter than a month.

Set C

In which seasons are these months?

1 February ________
2 March ________
3 April ________
4 May ________
5 June ________
6 July ________
7 August ________
8 October ________
9 November ________
10 December ________

Set D

What do these periods of time make?

1 365 days ________
2 12 months ________
3 7 days ________
4 28, 29, 30 or 31 days ________
5 2 terms ________
6 14 days ________
7 3 months ________
8 60 seconds ________
9 60 minutes ________
10 May, June, July ________

Set F

1 On my 10th birthday I will have lived for ___ months.

2 The footy finals are in September. This is in the season of ___.

3 ANZAC Day is in April in the season of ___.

4 The Olympics started on14 August and ended on 28 August. They lasted for a ____.

5 The Olympics lasted for ___ weeks.

6 My birthday is in February. This is in the season of ___.

7 25 December is Christmas Day. This is ___ days before the end of the month.

8 Year 3 lasts for ___ semesters.

9 I am 9, my sister is 7 and we were born on the same day of the year. I am ___ months older than her.

10 When I am 10, I will have lived for ___ weeks.

NSW: Measurement MS2.5; Qld: Measurement M3.2;
Vic: Measurement—Time 3.1; WA: Measurement M3.1; SA: Measurement 2.5

Measurement and Geometry

Unit 28 Money: Notes and coins

Our money system uses the 5-, 10-, 20- and 50-cent coins, the $1 and $2 coins and the $5, $10, $20, $50 and $100 notes.

Set A

Which coins feature:

1 **a platypus** ☐
2 **an echidna** ☐
3 **the coat of arms** ☐
4 **an Aboriginal elder** ☐
5 **a lyre bird** ☐
6 **an emu** ☐
7 **a person on each side** ☐
8 **1 kangaroo** ☐
9 **a mob of kangaroos** ☐
10 **not a circle** ☐

Set B

Find the right note:

1 **mainly blue** ☐
2 **mainly orange** ☐
3 **mainly green** ☐
4 **mainly pink** ☐
5 **mainly golden** ☐
6 **the most valuable** ☐
7 **the cheapest** ☐
8 **the biggest** ☐
9 **the smallest** ☐
10 **10 needed to make the most expensive note** ☐

Set E

Which notes and coins would be needed to make, as quickly as possible, these amounts of money:

1 **$5.20** ______________
2 **$6.50** ______________
3 **$7.00** ______________
4 **$8.10** ______________
5 **$9.50** ______________
6 **$11.00** ______________
7 **$12.40** ______________
8 **$14.00** ______________
9 **$15.50** ______________
10 **$18.00** ______________

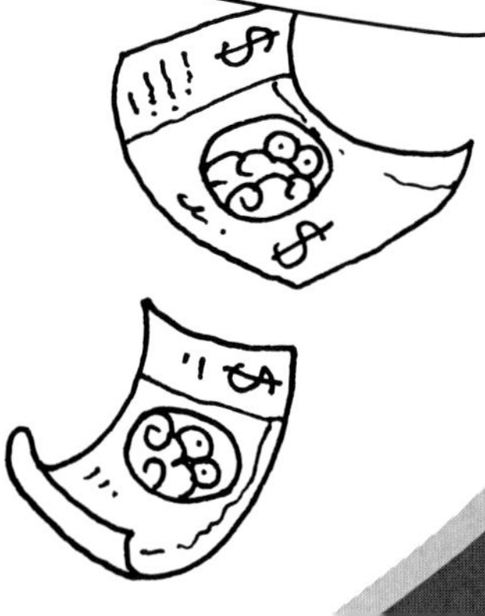

Set C

What is the smallest number of coins needed to make, as quickly as possible, these amounts of money:

1 **30c** ☐
2 **60c** ☐
3 **45c** ☐
4 **80c** ☐
5 **95c** ☐
6 **$1.20** ☐
7 **$1.55** ☐
8 **$2.50** ☐
9 **$4.00** ☐
10 **$4.85** ☐

Set D

What is the smallest number of notes needed to make, as quickly as possible, these amounts of money:

1 **$10** ☐
2 **$15** ☐
3 **$25** ☐
4 **$30** ☐
5 **$50** ☐
6 **$60** ☐
7 **$70** ☐
8 **$85** ☐
9 **$95** ☐
10 **$100** ☐

Set F

1 I have 3 coins with a platypus on them. I have _____ cents.

2 If these 3 coins had a mob of kangaroos on them, I would have ______.

3 In my purse I have 4 of the cheapest note. I have ______ altogether.

4 If I had 1 of every silver coin, I would have ______.

5 If I had 1 of every gold coin, I would have ______.

6 If I had 1 of every coin, I would have _______.

7 Which 2 coins feature the kangaroo? _____________

8 How many edges are on the 50c coin? ______

9 How many echidna coins make a dollar? ______

10 How many platypus coins make $2? ______

Number and Algebra

Unit 29 Money: Amounts, and adding and giving change

We need to be able to add and subtract money well to make sure we can shop effectively and to make sure we get the correct change when we buy things.

Set A

What change from $1 would I get if I spent:

1 50c ____
2 20c ____
3 10c ____
4 5c ____
5 90c ____
6 95c ____
7 80c ____
8 25c ____
9 15c ____
10 30c ____

Set B

What change from $2 would I get if I spent:

1 $1 ____
2 50c ____
3 $1.50 ____
4 $1.90 ____
5 10c ____
6 5c ____
7 $1.20 ____
8 90c ____
9 20c ____
10 $1.20 ____

Set E

What coins would I receive in change if I had $5 and spent:

1 $4 ______
2 $3 ______
3 $2 ______
4 $2.50 ______
5 $1 ______
6 $1.50 ______
7 $1.20 ______
8 50c ______
9 20c ______
10 5c ______

Set C

Add up the following coins:

1	5c + 10c	
2	20c + 20c	
3	20c + 10c + 5c	
4	50c + 20c	
5	50c + 20c + 10c	
6	$2 + 50c	
7	$2 + $1 + 50c	
8	$2 + $2 + 20c	
9	10c + 5c + $2	
10	50c + 50c + $2 + 20c	

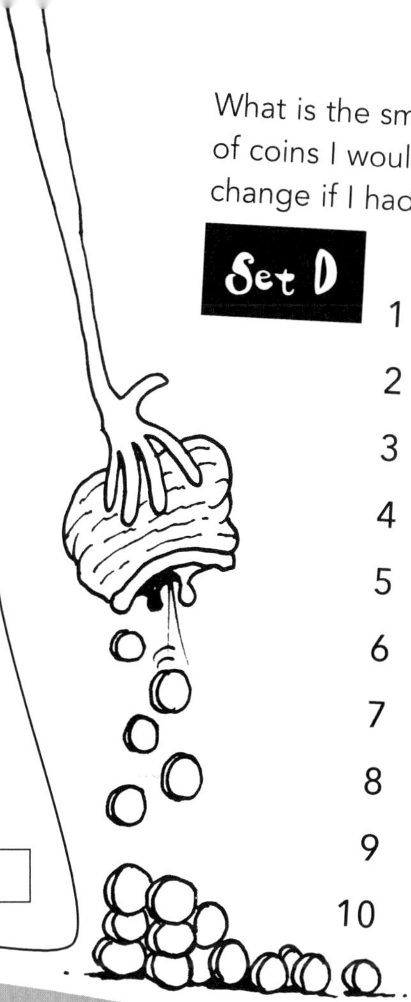

What is the smallest number of coins I would receive in change if I had $2 and spent:

Set D

1	$1	
2	$1.50	
3	$1.80	
4	$1.85	
5	$1.40	
6	$1.95	
7	50c	
8	90c	
9	40c	
10	20c	

Set F

1. If I had $5 and spent $3.50, my change would be ______.
2. This change should be in ____ coins.
3. If I had $2 and spent $1.10, my change would be ______.
4. This change should be in ____ coins.
5. If I had the coat of arms coin and spent 5c, my change would be ______
6. This change should be in ____ coins.
7. If I had $1 and spent 25c, my change would be ______.
8. The coins I should receive in my change would be ______________.
9. If I had the mainly pink note and spent the lyre bird coin, my change would be ______.
10. The coins I should receive in my change would be ____________________.

Measurement and Geometry

Unit 30 2D and 3D: Polygon and Polyhedra Properties

Two-dimensional shapes, called *polygons*, are flat and can be drawn easily on a piece of paper. Polygon comes from Greek and means 'many corners'.

Three-dimensional shapes, called *polyhedra*, have depth and can be picked up. Polyhedra comes from Greek and means 'many faces'.

Set A

How many sides can be found on these polygons:

1 **circle** ☐
2 **square** ☐
3 **rectangle** ☐
4 **rhombus** ☐
5 **oval** ☐
6 **pentagon** ☐
7 **hexagon** ☐
8 **octagon** ☐
9 **decagon** ☐
10 **triangle** ☐

Which 2D polygons can be found in these 3D polyhedra?

Set D

cube: 1 ______________

rectangular prism: 2 ______________ **and** 3 ______________

square pyramid: 4 ______________ **and** 5 ______________

triangular prism: 6 ______________ **and** 7 ______________

cylinder: 8 ______________ **and** 9 ______________

cone: 10 ______________

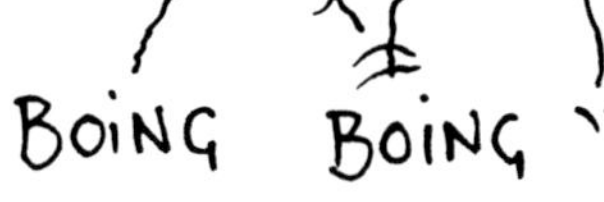

Set B

How many faces are on these polyhedra?

1 1 cube ☐
2 rectangular prism ☐
3 triangular prism ☐
4 sphere ☐
5 cylinder ☐
6 cone ☐
7 hexagonal prism ☐
8 square pyramid ☐
9 triangular pyramid ☐
10 hexagonal pyramid ☐

Set C

Find 10 examples of a rectangular prism in the room you are in now.

1 ____________
2 ____________
3 ____________
4 ____________
5 ____________
6 ____________
7 ____________
8 ____________
9 ____________
10 ____________

Set E

Name the polyhedra:

1 a cupboard ____________
2 a tennis ball ____________
3 a 6-sided die ____________
4 a water pipe ____________
5 a cricket ball ____________
6 a tissue box ____________
7 a 2-man tent ____________
8 a city building ____________
9 a pencil ____________
10 a book ____________

Set F

1 How many edges are on a cone? ____________
2 How many sides are on 5 hexagons? ____________
3 A ball is an example of a ____________.
4 A brick is an example of a ____________.
5 A toilet roll is an example of a ____________.
6 A cube has ______ corners.
7 7 equal shapes. 21 sides in total. Each is a ____________.
8 4 equal shapes. 24 corners in total. Each is a ____________.
9 A triangular prism is like a house's ________.
10 2 cubes stuck together make a ____________.

Statistics and Probability

Unit 31
Chance: Concepts of likelihood

The likelihood of something happening is the chance of it occurring. This can be said in words such as 'possible' and 'certain'. It can also be said as a fraction, like 3/5, which we read as '3 out of 5'.

Set A

Imagine you have a 6-sided die. Use the words 'possible', 'certain' or 'impossible' to describe the chance of rolling:

1 **a 2** ______________
2 **a 7** ______________
3 **an even number** ______________
4 **a fraction** ______________
5 **a number under 7** ______________
6 **an odd number** ______________
7 **1, 2, 3, 4 or 5** ______________
8 **a whole number** ______________
9 **a 2-digit number** ______________
10 **a decimal** ______________

Set D

If you tossed a coin the following number of times, how many heads do you think you might get?

1	**2**	
2	**6**	
3	**10**	
4	**14**	
5	**20**	
6	**22**	
7	**50**	
8	**100**	
9	**200**	
10	**1000**	

Set E

You have a 10-sided die. Answer as a fraction the chance of these results happening:

1 rolling a 10 _______
2 rolling a number bigger than 8 _____
3 rolling a 1 _______
4 rolling a 1 or a 10 _______
5 rolling an even number _____
6 rolling an odd number_______
7 rolling a 1, 2, 3 or 4 _______
8 rolling a 2, 4, 6, 8, 9 or 10 _______
9 rolling a number bigger than 1 _____
10 rolling a number smaller than 10 ______

Set B

With the same die, use the words 'likely' or 'unlikely' to describe the chance of rolling:

1 **a 5** ___________
2 **a 6** ___________
3 **1 or 2** ___________
4 **1, 2, 3 or 4** ___________
5 **1 or 6** ___________
6 **2, 3, 5 or 6** ___________
7 **1, 3, 5 or 6** ___________
8 **3 or 4** ___________
9 **2, 3, 4, 5 or 6** ___________
10 **a number bigger than 2** ___________

Set C

Answer as a fraction to show the chance of rolling these numbers on a 6-sided die:

1 **2** _____
2 **6** _____
3 **2 or 4** _____
4 **3 or 5** _____
5 **1 or 6** _____
6 **1, 2 or 3** _____
7 **3, 4 or 6** _____
8 **3, 4, 5 or 6** _____
9 **1, 2, 3, 4 or 5** _____
10 **2, 3, 4, 5 or 6** _____

Set F

1 Describe the chance that tomorrow the sun will come up. ___________
2 Describe the chance that it will rain in 3 days. ___________
3 Describe the chance that I will catch a cold next month. ___________
4 Describe the chance that the sun will rise in the west. ___________
5 What is the chance of rolling a 4 with a 6-sided die? _______
6 What is the chance of rolling a 4 with a 10-sided die? _______
7 What is the chance of tossing a tail with a 20 cent coin? _______
8 Describe the chance of seeing an echidna on the 50 cent coin. ___________
9 Describe the chance of seeing an echidna on the 5 cent coin. ___________
10 What is the chance of rolling an 8 with a 6-sided die? _______

Revision

Unit 32 Revision: All sorts

To finish the book, here are some revision questions that will cover all of the things you have worked through. Good luck!

Set A

1 10 = 4 + ☐
2 17 + 10 = ☐
3 8 + 11 = ☐
4 27 + 9 = ☐
5 10 – 7 = ☐
6 45 – 10 = ☐
7 56 – 11 = ☐
8 34 – 9 = ☐
9 double 13 ☐
10 halve 46 ☐

Set B

1 7 x 2 = ☐
2 3 x 8 = ☐
3 4 x 7 = ☐
4 7 x 5 = ☐
5 9 x 10 = ☐
6 24 ÷ 2 = ☐
7 12 ÷ 3 = ☐
8 44 ÷ 4 = ☐
9 60 ÷ 5 = ☐
10 80 ÷ 10 = ☐

Set E

1 How many lyre bird coins equal a dollar? ______

2 What is my change from $2 if I spend $1.75? ______

3 2 dollars equals ______ 10 cent coins.

4 A sugar cube has ______ faces.

5 3 decagons have ______ corners.

6 The chance of rolling an 8 with a 6-sided die is ______________.

7 The chance of the next number in the pattern 23, 25, 27, ... being 28 is ______________.

8 The chance of 33 244 being even is ____________.

9 The chance of a number in the 10 times table being even is ____________.

10 The chance of me getting all 10 of these questions correct is ____________.

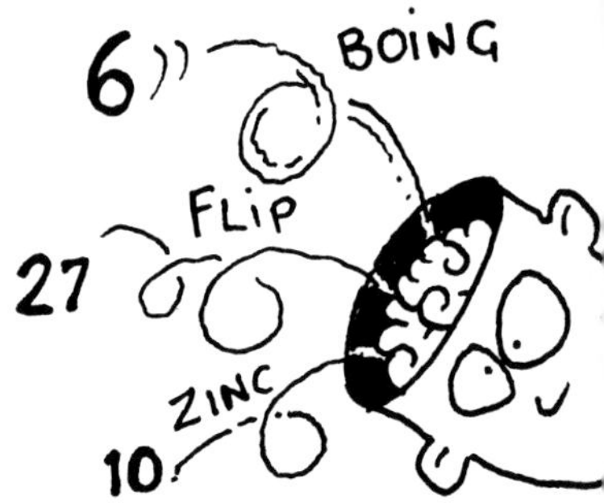

Set C

1 half of 22 ☐

2 a quarter of 16 ☐

3 the value of the 3 in 347 ☐

4 round 34 to the nearest 10 ☐

5 2, 5, 8, ☐ ,14

6 1, 2, 4, 8, ☐

7 12 + 8 – 4 = ☐

8 3 x 4 x 3 = ☐

9 25 ÷ 5 ÷ 1 = ☐

10 100 ÷ 10 ÷ 10 = ☐

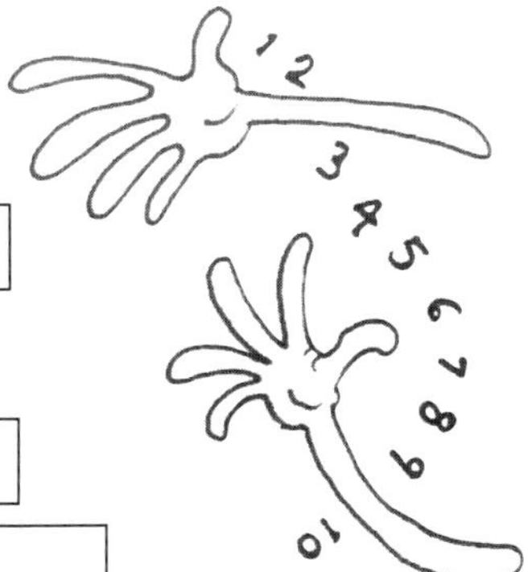

Set D

1 4 m = _____ cm

2 800 cm = ___ m

3 the perimeter of a square with sides 4 cm ______

4 2 kg = _____ g

5 7000 g = ___ kg

6 4 litres = ______ mL

7 11:05 = ____ past ____

8 days in June ______

9 At 7:40 the big hand is on the ____

10 36 months = ____ years

Set F

1 What is the 7th odd number? _____

2 What is the 7th even number? _____

3 Find the difference between 2 x 2 and 3 x 3. _____

4 What day comes 5 days after Saturday? _____________

5 How many coins equal $3.30? _____

6 I have 7 equal shapes that have 35 sides altogether. They are ____________.

7 Round 255 to the nearest 100. _____

8 How many of the cheapest silver coin equal the cheapest gold coin? _____

9 Find the product of 5 and 10 and 2. _____

10 How many times can 4 be taken away from 32? _____

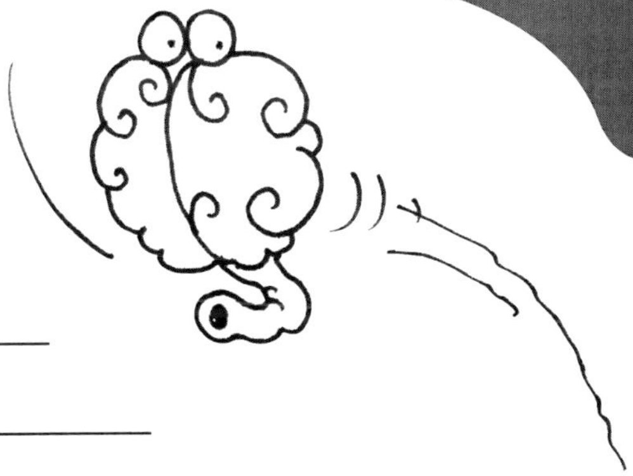

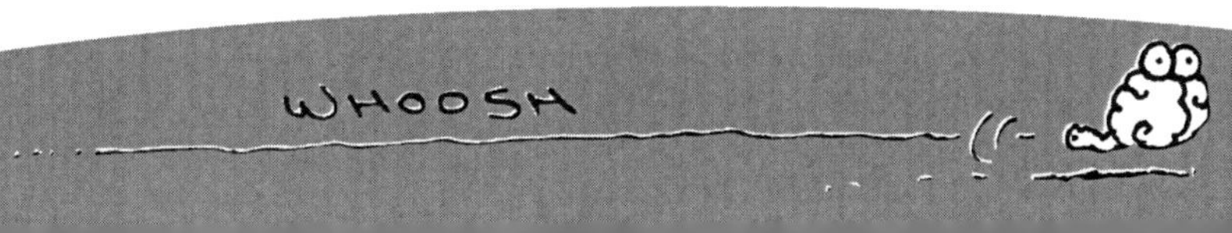

Glossary

Add	To group together
Altogether	The answer to an addition problem
Analogue clock	A sweep-hand clock
Autumn	March, April, May
Bi	A prefix meaning 2
Centi	A prefix meaning $\frac{1}{100}$
Centimetre	100th of a metre
Deca	A prefix meaning 10
Decade	A period of 10 years
Decagon	A 10-sided shape
Difference	How far one number is away from another number
Divide	To split up into equal pieces or to share
Double	To add a number onto itself
Dozen	12
Edge	A boundary
Face	A side of a 3D shape
Gram	The standard unit for mass
Groups of	Counting in lots
Halve	Divide into 2 equal parts
Heptagon	A shape with 7 sides
Hexagon	A shape with 6 sides
Kilo	A prefix meaning 1000
Kilogram	1000 grams
Kilometre	1000 metres
Litre	The standard unit of capacity
Margin	How far 2 numbers are apart
Metre	The standard unit of length
Millilitre	One thousandth of a litre
Multiply	Count groups
Octa	A prefix meaning 8
Octagon	A shape with 8 sides
Penta	A prefix meaning 5
Pentagon	A polygon with 5 sides
Perimeter	The length of the boundary of a shape
Polygon	A 2D shape with many corners
Polyhedra	A 3D shape with many faces
Product	The answer to a multiplication problem
Quad	A prefix meaning 4
Quadrilateral	A 4-sided shape
Quadruple	To multiply by 4
Quotient	The result of a division question
Regular (shape)	Having the same side lengths
Remainder	What is left over after a division sum has been completed
Remove	To take away
Round	To take a number to the nearest 10, 100, 1000 etc
Rule	The pattern in a sequence
Sequence	A number pattern
Share	To divide into equal pieces
Solve	To find the answer to a question
Spring	September, October, November
Subtract	Take away
Sum	The answer to an addition problem
Summer	December, January, February
Term	Each member of a sequence
Times	Groups of
Total	The answer to an addition problem
Tri	A prefix meaning 3
Triple	To multiply by 3
Twice	2 times, or to double
Vertice	The corner where lines meet on 2D or 3D shapes
Winter	June, July, August